What He Did for Love

What He Did for Love

A Companion for the Forty Days of Lent

Francis X. Gaeta

Foreword by Thelma Hall, r.c.

Resurrection Press
Mineola • New York

*Dedicated with
love and deep affection
to my Bishop John McGann
who shows me and countless others
what it means to be a good shepherd
and to love one's little flock.*

First published in February, 1998 by Resurrection Press, Ltd.
P.O. Box 248, Williston Park, NY
11596

Copyright © 1998 by Francis X. Gaeta

ISBN 1-878718-41-X
Library of Congress Catalog Card Number 97-075613

Cover photo and design by John Murello.
Photo from Immaculate Conception Center, Douglaston, NY.

Illustrations on pages 12 and 13 are from the *Daily Roman Missal*, Scepter Publishers, copyright 1993 Fr. James Socias, and are used with permission.

Printed in the United States of America.

CONTENTS

Foreword

IN 1966, AS A SISTER OF THE CENACLE, my home was the Cenacle Retreat House in Lake Ronkonkoma, Long Island. By a happy coincidence the superior of that community was Rita Hudlin. We had first met as retreatants there, years before either of us entered the Cenacle, and now, on a significant day in my life in 1966, she came running up the stairs to my room in great excitement, saying, "Thelma! You've got to come down and meet this new priest! He's just made a Cursillo and he's on fire!"

The new priest was Frank Gaeta, and that fire is still burning high! Indeed, as a reader of his book, you will experience its light and warmth, as this man in love with God shares that love throughout these pages.

This is a book not only for the season of Lent. It also reveals an Incarnational spirituality leading to action. It provides a way to *pray* Scripture, and a new view of "fasting" in company with joy. Fr. Frank's goal is, simply, to help us become more loving by perpetuating the life of Jesus in and through us, here and now.

Lent is seen here as a gifted time to grow in intimacy with Jesus, rediscovering what we already possess: the life of God in us. It offers us new perspectives on loving ourselves as we are, "warts and all," *unconditionally* loved by God.

Lent here is revealed as a constantly renewed opportunity to see how our ordinary everyday living, our contacts with others, our failures—all—can be the means to allow God to love us into new life.

And always, we find compassion, for here is a Jesus of total availability. Here is a passion for life, opening our eyes and hearts to the ubiquitous presence of a Jesus present in all the ordinariness of our days, and above all, in ourselves. Here the historical times of Jesus are translated, from the distance of centuries, into our immediate situations and encounters.

This is not Fr. Frank "preaching at us," but sharing our common human weaknesses and frailties, made newly recognizable as *opportunities* to "open one's heart to the grace and power of God's love" and to an experience of resurrection, always here and now.

Perhaps the single most effective gift of this small book is its everydayness, which teaches a genuine Christ-centered spirituality. "Christians have to be taught to *expect* the experience of the living God in their prayer life and daily living.... What is needed is a giant leap beyond the safe prayers that are limited to books and other people's words. We need to propel ourselves into the holy place and it is there that we will find God." (Page 36)

On every page we are called past the conventional (and unfortunately often literal and impersonal) aspect of Scripture, to its clear and intimate relevance to our own everyday lives.

Having completed the reading, praying and living of this book, one will have learned how Scripture when prayed from the heart, can lead to a greater love of others and, equally important, of ourselves. It is not only about the Passion of Jesus but about what life can mean when we allow ourselves to live and love passionately, for:

"Our greatest challenge in Lent will be to accept [God's] gift of love" [offered to us] "without price or condition. It is ours for the taking." (Page 51)

THELMA HALL, r.c.

Introduction

My Dear Friend:

I am so happy that we will be walking together on this Lenten journey. The Forty Days is a special time of grace for Christians to pay more attention to our spiritual life and our journey to God.

This little book is meant to do two things: first, to draw us closer to the word of God each day, especially the Gospel; and then to encourage us to pray about our *Daily Bread*, the *Living Word of God*. The daily meditations are meant to be springboards to personal prayer. Each day, hopefully, each of us will be writing and speaking our own prayers and meditations as we respond to the word.

Scripture is the real source book for Lenten prayer. Each day the Scriptures read at Mass will be cited. The meditations will focus on the Gospel (Cycle A). Read the word slowly and pause at any words, phrases, or images that touch you. Speak to the Lord about them. Rest in the peace of the Lord as you feel touched by His presence.

As you read the meditations, perhaps there will be other areas of conversation with the Lord that will be suggested. Follow them and pray through them. But remember, the best prayer is what will flow from our own hearts and personal experiences. No one else can do our praying or loving for us. We must do it ourselves. The Holy Spirit will guide us.

What this book is meant to do is to bring us to the word of God each day for fifteen minutes. In that period of time we will be allowing the Lord to gently touch our hearts and teach us how to pray. We will be in the process of conversion which is what Lent is all about. We will be preparing to renew our life with the Lord at the beautiful moment of the renewal of the Baptismal Promises at Easter Mass.

I hope and pray that this Lenten practice will help you to begin a habit of daily Scripture reading and prayer, stimulate your present prayer life, or renew an old practice that perhaps you've neglected.

Lent is a wonderful opportunity to begin all over again. The ashes on Ash Wednesday remind us of our death, it is true, but they do that only to assure us of the new life that is ours for the asking. Lent and Good Friday only have meaning because Jesus is risen from the dead. Our Lenten observance will help us to enter again into the mystery of Jesus—His death and resurrection—and ours.

Together we will journey from the ashes of Ash Wednesday to the flames of the new paschal fire. We will journey with Jesus as He leads us through the Paschal Mystery of His death and Resurrection. Let us pray for one another as we walk together with Jesus to the new life He promises us.

In Jesus' love,

Frank

Fast from...

discontent
anger
bitterness
self-concern
despair
guilt
suspicion
laziness

Feast on...

gratitude
forgiveness
compassion
hope
commitment
truth
patience
the mercy of God

1.

Lent Is a Time for Fasting

WE ALWAYS THINK of the word fasting in connection with Lent. Lent has always meant denying ourselves candy, movies, television, pizza, beer, etc. When we were little children some beautiful Christ figure in our lives suggested "giving up" something for Lent. Indeed, Jesus Himself goes into the desert for forty days to fast. Fasting, by choice or by law, has been part of our Lenten and Christian experience for two thousand years. Far be it from me to minimize it or downplay it, but *why* do we fast? *What* should we be fasting from?

We fast to remind ourselves that we have to be in control of ourselves and that no "thing" should ever dominate our lives. In Lent, as we do our soul-searching to prepare ourselves for Easter, we may decide that we are eating or drinking too much, looking at too much television, or even killing ourselves by smoking. Our Lenten fast is then a way of restoring right order to our lives.

We might also look to fasting as a way of praying and praising the Lord. Our fast then becomes a way of saying that the Lord Jesus is more important than any creature. We love the Lord more than any of His creatures no matter how good or how beautiful they might be in themselves. These motives for fasting are compelling in an Incarnational spirituality which views using creation properly as the greatest of all prayers to honor the Creator.

Fasting should be medicinal in the sense that it

restores good health to parts of our spirit that are troubled or sick. The gossiper tries to be quiet. The glutton practices moderation. The lazy person becomes more motivated and concerned about serving others.

Fasting is also a means of bringing us closer to Jesus in His agony and passion. Fasting brings us closer to the Jesus who dies that we might live. We nail to the cross of Jesus those parts of our hearts that are not yet fully redeemed and do not yet belong to His kingdom. We allow them to die so that we might live a new life.

Fasting also brings us closer to the poor and the suffering. In some small way we experience what the majority of our sisters and brothers are *always* living: hunger, pain and deprivation. In our little inconveniences that we call "fasting," we become united with the Christ Who is *always* fasting and *always* in pain—His poor. This Lenten pain compels us to work for peace and justice so that their eternal Lent might come to an end and that they might experience the Lord's resurrection in this life as well as in the next.

The above may be of some help in determining *how* we fast to get into spiritual shape. It will range from getting up on time to giving up dessert. Only Jesus and I know what I need. Each of us must be the doctor of our own soul along with Jesus.

Fast we must. Everyone must fast from *bitterness,* from *self-concern,* from *despair,* from *guilt,* from *suspicion,* from *anger,* from *laziness,* from *pettiness.* The list of those things that the Lord would have us fast from is *very* long.

One final thought on fasting...

Just be sure that if it's laziness or discontent you should be fasting from, that you don't give up smoking because that's what you've done for the last twenty years! The fast you choose should result in making you more loving and more like Jesus. Otherwise, it's a waste of time.

2.

Lent Is a Time for Feasting

WE SELDOM THINK of the word feasting in connection with Lent, but there is no word more appropriate to describe the works of the Holy Spirit in our hearts in this holy season.

It is a time to feast on the goodness and mercy of God and a time to be lavish in sharing these gifts with ourselves and with the world. It is a time to luxuriate in the love of our God. *"God so loved the world He gave His only begotten Son" (John 3:16).* These words are at the very heart of Lent. We are led into the desert to renew the marriage covenant of our Lover and ourselves. He/She lures us into the desert almost seducing us to believe and accept the passionate love and tenderness that our God has for us.

Let us not be distracted by the somberness of the Lenten purple. The time of Lent is the great time of passion and renewal of our love affair with Love. It is as much the time to accept, to embrace and to celebrate as it is to deny and to give up or let go. The prayerful reading of the Book of Hosea describes in powerful images the movement of the God-Lover to renew the love covenant that has been broken by the adulterous spouse (you and me). The great feast of Lent is meant for us to celebrate and renew our love for our God, beginning with the renewal of our love of ourselves. This love that we celebrate with ourselves and our Lover will naturally overflow to everyone in our lives.

The great feast of Lent grows from our feasting on the Love of God. It grows into a feast of *gratitude* as our hearts praise the Lord for all the blessings in our lives. We feast on *forgiveness* as we forgive ourselves and all who have hurt us through our lives. We believe in the total forgiveness won for us on the cross.

Our feasting is filled with *compassion* as we have a new heart for the suffering and pain of the human family. We see humanity on the cross with Jesus and we have a new heart to work for social justice and peace. Our feasting gives us a new *hope* as we believe in the goodness of our world and the goodness of people. We feast on the hope that we can grow and change for the better.

Our feasting has generous portions of *commitment* as we say our "yes" once again to the Lord and to the call He has given to us. We want to be the best husband, wife, parent, sister, brother or friend that we can be.

Our feasting is a sharing in the *truth* of Jesus as we give our lives as Jesus did for what is just and right. We take a stand based on truth and conscience and we stick with it.

The great feast is a feast of *patience*. We know that growth in ourselves takes time, just as it does in other people and institutions. This patience can never be an excuse for laziness or indifference, but a real acceptance of our frailty and the need to believe, encourage, and challenge ourselves and others.

Our great feast is always topped off by generous doses of the *mercy of God*. We celebrate and feast on that great mercy. It is our hope for the present and the future. It is our celebrating of the God of Love, the Passionate One, whose very being is to love and to forgive—that Great Lover who will never withdraw His promise or His invitation to the abundant Feast of Life.

Lent is also the great feasting time of renewing our love for one another. It is a time to join in the banquet of friendship, family and love. We should be filled with many good things as we celebrate Easter.

3.

Lent Is a Time of Conversion

IN EVERY PARISH during Lent the community becomes acquainted with those who will be baptized or make their profession of faith at the Easter Vigil. At the Sunday liturgy, the candidates go through the public Rites on their way to becoming part of the family. It is always a touching experience to witness the gift of faith as it begins to flower in their hearts.

As they receive the Scriptures, the Creed, the Lord's Prayer, and as they sign on the dotted line in the Book of the Elect, we cannot help but think about our own journey to God and our own need for conversion.

We describe ourselves as Catholics or Christians and that is not true. We are only in the *process* of becoming Christians. There is never a time when we are finished or the journey completed. Our whole life is a process and a journey of becoming another Christ. Each stage of our life holds the possibility and promise of deeper growth and deeper understanding.

Our relationship with Jesus must always be growing. We do not "practice" our faith as if it were a skill we possess and use for the rest our life. We are always in the process of learning what it all means and that knowledge and understanding changes as we change. The ability of a parent to understand the love of the *God-Parent* will be much more intense as that parent holds his/her newborn child compared to when that parent was a teenager. Every experience and every person we meet will in some way change our ability to respond to God's call and will call us to respond in a different way.

The catechumens will force us to reflect upon our own faith and force us to ask ourselves some pointed questions about our response to God. They will challenge us to look into our hearts and to question ourselves about how we have used the gifts that this loving God has given us. How different is the world because of me? How much better is my family and my parish because of me?

The RCIA candidates will make us squirm a bit as they embrace Jesus with such joy and enthusiasm. They will make us yearn for the certainty and the exuberance of the faith of our youth. They will also reassure us that what the Lord gives them He has already given to us in abundance. He is just waiting for us to ask Him for the Holy Spirit to ignite our faith into the fire of His Love.

Conversion isn't just about Jews, Protestants or agnostics becoming Catholics. It is much more about Catholics becoming Christians, other Christs. Becoming Christian is the process of accepting and living all the wonderful gifts that our God has already given to us. There's nothing new the Lord has to give us, but living what He has already given us will make all things new.

4.

Lent Is a Time
to Embrace the Cross

LENT IS A TIME to come to terms with the cross. Each of us has a cross that we must carry. Some of these crosses come to us because of circumstances in our lives and events beyond our control. We have all dealt with the sickness or death of a loved one. We have all been there for a friend who has suffered an emotional crisis in his/her life. The cross is no stranger to a disciple of Jesus, indeed He tells us that we must take up our cross daily and follow him. At times like that we are able to unite ourselves with the sufferings of the Lord on the cross so we can get through them.

But life and the cross are very unfair. Some people seem to carry crosses that are disproportionately heavy and difficult. Some people never seem to get out from under the weight of their cross. For some it seems that their lives are meant to be nothing but suffering and pain.

There are so many people in unhappy marriages. All the joy and peace that this sacrament is meant to give them is denied them. It's not usually a question of fault or blame, just that people grow apart and before they realize it, they are strangers who cannot become friends. It's not just a question of problems that can be worked out through therapy. That would be easy. It is beyond that. There is no working them out. They live together to maintain a place of love for their children. They give their lives as a very special gift of love that we seldom speak about: being unhappy with a spouse but doing everything they can to seem happy for the sake of the children. These people are saints. They are so holy and close to Jesus as He suffers on the cross. They suffer with Him. They will also rise with Him. But not yet.

Other holy people cannot stay in a marriage. They opt for divorce and single parenthood because they feel it is the only alternative they have for the good of their children. So many of these beautiful people gave everything they had to make a marriage work, but it wasn't enough to save it. They mourn for that loss and failure and sometimes look upon themselves as failures when in reality they are saints. So many suffer all through their lives for choices they made when they were young and immature. They pay for them and wonder why they can't have a life like other people—a life of happiness and peace.

Parents who love children and who watch them suffer or even die can never erase that memory from their hearts. There will always be a part of them that is dead and in pain. The lover goes through life knowing that there cannot be a complete healing, because love and blood are too deep and too precious. There simply are wounds that cannot, and will not, ever be fully healed.

For some the cross is always present. They feel abandoned and alone. To those we've named one can add the gay person, the disabled, the person with AIDS or cancer, the unhappy priest or nun, the unfulfilled single person. The list is endless. They feel unimportant, discarded, and that they really don't belong.

During Lent all those special and beloved friends of Jesus must look at the cross and believe that Jesus loves them. They must be converted to know that Jesus bears their pain and that Jesus is there for them to have life and hope. They are called to embrace Jesus and to know that He shares their pain and that He is always there for them and suffering with them.

Jesus is never more a Savior than to those who yearn for and need salvation most. Jesus loves those who are in agony with a tender and total love. Jesus holds them in His arms and never lets go. Lent calls them to embrace the Savior who is always there for them.

In the process of our personal salvation, we who experience the saving mercy of Jesus become savior and healer to others. Jesus uses us to be the instruments of His peace and mercy. As we die with Him we bring new life to others through Him.

5.

Proper Readings of Lent

Ash Wednesday and the Beginning of Lent
Joel 2:12-18, 2 Corinthians 5:20–6:2
Matthew 6: 1-6, 16-18

THE FIRST FOUR DAYS of Lent set the theme for the entire holy season. We begin with the ancient and somewhat puzzling ritual of the imposition of the blessed ashes on our foreheads on Ash Wednesday. The Church is telling us something we are not happy to hear: we shall all die—we are mortal. Our bodies will decay and turn to dust.

The Church is asking us in this ritual if we are ready to go home. Are we? Lent is the time to get ready to "pack our bags" as Pope John referred to it. We have to go beyond the popular hype of today that loves to speculate about the End Times, the Rapture and the third millennium. Put simply, the Christian is called to live each day as if it were his/her last, and never fear death. We must be ready to meet our Jesus tonight if He calls us home. The time of Lent is meant to convert us to a deeper love of Jesus. In Lent our catechumens and candidates prepare for Baptism and reception into the Church. The rest of us prepare for the renewal of our Baptismal Promises at Easter.

The Church traditionally suggests three ways to achieve this transformation: *prayer, fasting* and *works of love.*

The *prayer* that we are called to in Lent is not the prayer of words or formulas or even liturgy. We are called to the prayer of the heart. This kind of prayer flows from the loving relationship we have with our God—our Lover—the author of all life and love. It is prayer that flows from an attitude of belonging to and being held by Mother/Father who loves us beyond all things. On Tuesday of the first week of Lent, we will reflect more on this Prayer of the Heart.

Fasting is an invitation to do something that will heal our hearts and our emotions. But we have to be our own doctor. No one knows what area of fasting we need more than we do ourselves. Perhaps our language has become vulgar and we need to correct ourselves so that we talk like a Christian! Perhaps we have to work on being kind to someone. Perhaps we are addicted to TV, food, drink, etc., and we know we have to restore our freedom in these areas. Perhaps we know that we need psychological counseling. What a great fast it would be to begin that journey! Maybe our fasting is joining a Twelve Step Program to achieve freedom and liberation. Perhaps fasting means taking care of ourselves physically, emotionally or spiritually.

Whatever the fast consists of, we do it in union with the Passion of Jesus on the cross and in union with the multitudes of our sisters and brothers who are *always* fasting because they are poor. Be your own doctor and write your own prescription that will bring new health this Lent.

Works of mercy and love are always the fruit of holiness. We have to grow in love for one another as we grow in love for the Lord. Lent is meant to deepen the bonds of family and friendship so that we are truly His Body touching the world with compassion and gentle mercy. Lent is a time for love to express itself in reconciliation. There are six weeks of Lent. How about writing the numbers one to six on a piece of paper and next to each number write the name of someone you've hurt or neglected. Call one of those people each week—renew love and friendship—get together with that person to celebrate the Eucharist of love and friend-ship. What a blessing that would be for the Church!

Jesus calls us into the desert this Lent. He invites us to renew the covenant of love. He whispers in our ears words of love, hoping that we will fall in love again and renew the marriage covenant of our Baptism by loving Him with all our hearts. Our Spouse/Lover has always been faithful, and now He invites us to renew our love and fidelity. For the Israelites the desert reminds them of the "honeymoon" with God when they had no cities, no armies, no temple—just Yahweh. And so again this Lent, Yahweh lures us into the desert of our hearts where He will speak tender words of love to us. It's time to heed His call and follow Him into the desert and to allow Him to love us.

Thursday After Ash Wednesday
Deuteronomy 30:15-20, Psalm 1: 1-2, 3, 4, 6
Luke 9: 22-25

WE ARE ALREADY THINKING about the Passion in today's Gospel. Already we have to deal with the folly and contra-diction of the cross. Only from death will new life come; only in losing my life will I be able to find it. Only in self denial will I be able to grow into my true and real person-hood.

The cross turns everything in the world and in my life upside-down! What I think is wise turns out to be foolish. What I think is important really is superficial. What I pour out my energy and hard work on is often very trifling in the kingdom and under the sign of the cross. The cross will force me to see that I am spiritually insane. Lent is the time to regain my wits by putting everything right side up.

How *does* Jesus look at my career, my marriage, my priesthood, my relationships, my use of money and things? Do my life and values reflect the ideals of Jesus or are they simply a reflection of the values of society?

This conversion stuff is tough work! It's putting things back where they belong. It's looking at all reality with the mind and heart of Jesus. It's saying that I'm wrong and I have to begin again. It's acknowledging that I don't know anything and I better go to the One who does. That's what Lent is all about! It's much more than giving up cake or beer!

Friday After Ash Wednesday
Isaiah 58:1-9, Psalm 51: 3-4, 5-6, 18-19
Matthew 9:14-15

TODAY'S GOSPEL speaks of two topics that are at the heart of Christianity—*feasting* and *fasting*. They are a big part of our own lives, or at least they should be. Jesus is criticized because he was always feasting. His main vehicle of evangelization was table ministry. He was constantly accepting invitations to dinner from everybody, the rich and poor and the saints and sinners. He sat down at anyone's table so that they could experience first hand the presence of God's love and call in their lives. Fasting was also part of the life of Jesus.

The desert experience was very important for His preparation for ministry. There were many times that He had to be alone to pray and fast. Unfortunately, in our own lives we've lost the ability to really feast or to truly fast. Somewhere in the middle we find ourselves doing neither, but operating on automatic pilot in which we allow our calendars to consume our days to the point of not really doing anything with any gusto or fervor.

There are times when we *should* feast. There are times when we should pull out all the stops and celebrate with our beloved family and friends. Often that celebration includes great food and drink, but the most important element is the feast of our time and total presence to the people we love. A wonderful Lenten practice could be to have a special dinner and a good bottle of wine with a dear friend. But we also need the fasting. We need the time to be alone with the Lord. We need that quiet time to pray and sort out all the pieces of our lives.

Only when we learn to fast are we able to feast, and only feasting makes fasting special. Lent is a time to learn how to fast and how to feast. In the process we bring real passion back into our lives.

Saturday after Ash Wednesday
Isaiah 58:9-14, Psalm 86:1-2, 3-4, 5-6
Luke 5:27-32

JESUS SPEAKS TO LEVI as he collects his taxes: "Follow me." And Levi does! Levi gets up and leaves it all behind–career, prestige, security and common sense. He walks away from what is safe and certain and throws a party for Jesus to celebrate what has just happened to him—he has found meaning and purpose in his life. He has found Jesus.

Jesus is calling me to follow Him. He's inviting me to live in a new way in which I depend upon Him rather than on my own control and manipulation. He's calling me to take more chances and not to be afraid of risks or making mistakes. He's calling me to make a fool of myself once in a while, rather than always needing to be safe and right.

Levi gives up a great deal when he leaves his safe and respected tax station. So do we when we're willing to go into areas where Jesus is calling us. We begin to know the excitement of allowing Jesus to lead us rather than our trying to control and contain Jesus. We enter a new terrain when we allow the Holy Spirit to have a real part in our decisions and goals.

Life led by the Holy Spirit is never predictable. It is

always new. It can never be boring, and it will always surprise us. Lent is a wonderful time to ask the Holy Spirit what is really important. What should I be doing with my life? Are my priorities those of the Lord?

Jesus is saying: "Follow me!" Do I have the courage to try?

FIRST SUNDAY OF LENT
Deuteronomy 26:4-10, Romans 10:8-13
Luke 4:1-13

JESUS IS LED by the Spirit into the desert where He is tempted by the devil. I don't know why, but I always felt that the temptations Jesus endured in the desert were the only ones He faced in His life. I've come to see it in a new way. The whole of His life was filled with temptation to move away from His Father and to choose what *He* wanted over what the Spirit was calling Him to.

The life of Jesus is so much like ours. He is constantly being tempted to live for Himself instead of His Father. Jesus deals with discouragement, sadness, hostility, homesickness, misunderstanding and false judgments on the part of others. Jesus knows loneliness, fatigue, hurt, depression and anger. There are moments when he would like to leave it all, find someone to share His life with or just be left alone. Jesus is like us in *all* things, but sin.

As great as the temptation may become, Jesus opts for His Father's Love. But Jesus, our Brother, knows our pain. He knows our struggles and He knows our failures. He is never more our Savior than when we are tempted and when we fall. He is always there to lift us up again, to encourage us and to assure us that we are forgiven. We are forgiven by a brother who *knows* the pain we endure in our temptations. In this time of Lent, He assures us He is always with us and He tells us He believes in us and that we must never give up because He is there for us. He reminds us that we are His saints. What is a saint? A saint is a sinner who keeps on trying and *never* gives up!

Monday of the First Week of Lent
Leviticus 19:1-2,11-18, Psalm 19:8, 9, 10, 15
Matthew 25:31-46

MATTHEW 25 sets the scene of the Final Judgment. It is one that gives us pause in the early part of Lent because it really sets the tone for all of Lent. In it, Jesus identifies Himself totally and completely with the poor. "*I* was hungry; *I* was thirsty; *I* was a stranger; *I* was naked; *I* was in prison; *I* was ill." "Whatsoever you do to the least of my brothers and sisters you do to Me."

As we follow Jesus into the desert of this Lent, He invites us to look at humanity in a new way. The face of the person who annoys us or even persecutes us is the face of Jesus. He calls us to a new compassion for all people. He calls us to a new tolerance and a new way of forgiveness. In this time of Lent we are called to love and forgive in a way that we have never done before—from the heart—believing that each person—the good and the bad—is truly Christ.

As we touch Jesus in the Eucharist, so do we touch Him in the people in our lives—especially those who think differently than we do, those who rub us the wrong way and those whom we don't like.

Who is Jesus inviting us to touch this Lent? Who are the people we look through, or ignore or dismiss? Who are the people in whose eyes we fail to see pain or brokenness? Who are the people whom we treat as non-persons? They are Christ.

Tuesday of the First Week of Lent
Isaiah 55:10-11, Psalm 34:4-5, 6-7, 16-17, 18-19
Matthew 6: 7-15

TODAY, JESUS TEACHES US how to pray. Unfortunately, we have made too much of the words of the Our Father and we have forgotten that what Jesus teaches us is *not* the words of a prayer but *how* to pray. Jesus is teaching us the Prayer of the Heart—a way of praying and relating to our Father that flows from faith in His unconditional love for us. This kind of prayer is possible only when we know how much He loves us. It occurs as we begin to understand that the Father delights in us, that we are His beloved children and that He only wants the best for us. This kind of prayer happens when we see ourselves comfortable and at peace in the arms of the Father who loves us. We know that His love is ours even though we could never earn it or deserve it. It is pure gift.

The unconditional, total and pure love of parents holding a newborn infant in their arms is only a hint of how much our God—our Mother/Father—loves us. When we begin to know and accept that love, we begin to pray the Prayer of the Heart. This prayer doesn't depend upon right words or methods. It is, rather, a prayer that flows from the knowledge that we are in the arms of the One who loves us the most and in those arms there really is little that needs to be said except to say, "I love you."

Lent is the time to go beyond words, phrases, techniques and methods of prayer and to begin really to pray. When we truly believe in that love, then we can begin to pray.

Wednesday of the First Week of Lent
Jonah 3:1-10, Psalm 51:3-4, 12-13, 18-19
Luke 11:29-32

"YOU HAVE ONE greater than Solomon or Jonah here." In today's Gospel Jesus laments the fact that He's not good enough to convince His people. They want, they demand a sign. We are so much like them. We have *everything*. There is nothing more the Lord can give to us. Yet how little we really accept and believe. We take things so matter-of-fact-ly. Seldom do we *really* hear the Scriptures. So often, it's in one ear and out the other. "I've heard that Gospel before, what can it teach *me*?" So often I say my *'Amen'* at Communion not as an acclamation of faith and commit-ment, but as a safe and sanitary liturgical response that says nothing and means nothing. Even the Eucharist becomes ordinary and predictable when it should be the most revo-lutionary moment of my life. The Eucharist demands response, conversion and charity toward all people. I make it a pious and safe moment of quiet consolation rather than a *call* and *response to discipleship and service*. How often I con-fess my sins without weeping for what I have done or failed to do to the Body of Christ! How often I act as if my sins were virtues rather than offenses against the love that God has poured out upon me. And yes, I look at the crucifix and I'm so used to it that I don't see His suffering as the greatest act of love the world has ever known. Lent is so much about opening my eyes and seeing the reality around me, and understanding it for the first time.

Thursday of the First Week of Lent
Esther C. 12, 14-16, 23-25, Psalm 138:1-3, 7-8
Matthew 7:7-12

"DO UNTO OTHERS as you would have them do unto you." Jesus tells us that the Golden Rule summarizes the Lord and the prophets. Think of what a marvelous rule of life Jesus has given to us. It is practical, home-spun, earthy spir-ituality. It is the basic common sense holiness and wisdom of the plain folk who know how to live their lives.

What a world we could live in if we followed the Golden Rule—think of it! I would never do, say or think anything about another person unless I wanted the same done to me. Think of what would happen in marriages when spouses began to act this way toward each other. Think about what would happen in home, school and places of work! Think of what would happen if the world, with its war, racism, genocide and terrorism, began living out the Golden Rule. We would truly be living in the Kingdom of God if individuals and nations lived this way.

Think of your own life and how differently you would treat and speak to the members of your family and all your acquaintances. How gentle, understanding, compassionate and forgiving you would become as you tried to live the Golden Rule. What a different person you would become and what a different world it would be if we did unto others as we would have them do unto us. What a beautiful Lent we will have as we try to live this way!

Friday of the First Week of Lent
Ezekiel 18:21-28, Psalm 130:1-2, 3-4, 4-6, 7-8
Matthew 5:20-26

"LEAVE YOUR GIFT at the altar and go to be reconciled with your brother." This command of Jesus is so obvious and so powerful. No doubt about it, it *is* easier to offer the gift at the altar than to go and be reconciled with our sister or brother. Liturgy and form are always easier than relationship and life. It is scandalous, but true: many Christians celebrate liturgy and worship their God with hearts that are twisted with hatred and alienation toward their own flesh and blood.

In so many otherwise good families there are relationships that have been allowed to wither away and die because of some disagreement or hurt—frequently over money! Sometimes nothing can be done about it, but many times a loving and compassionate Christian can begin the process of healing, forgiveness and reconciliation with that famous and indispensable *first* phone call.

Who am I being called to reach out to this Lent? How can I begin a new chapter in the history of my family or of a relationship? That phone call I make literally has the power to change someone's heart. What an incredible Jesus moment it is when I dial that phone number and begin again. The butterflies in my stomach and the nervousness disappear when I hear my friend's voice at the other end, and a new chapter begins in my life. "Go first and be reconciled." You just can't beat that advice.

Saturday of the First Week of Lent
Deuteronomy 26:16-19, Psalm 119:1-2, 4-5, 7-8
Matthew 5: 43-48

JESUS CALLS US TODAY to perfection—to love our enemies and to pray for our persecutors. He calls us to forgive those who have hurt us. He calls us to a completely new way of life that goes totally against the grain of human nature. We have to know that we cannot do these things by mere willpower. We require the power of God's love—the Holy Spirit—to love our enemies and to forgive our persecutors. We simply cannot do it on our own.

Is it really possible to forgive a murderer, a rapist, a child abuser, a terrorist? I know *I* couldn't do it on my own, by my own willing it. When one is confronted with the unforgivable in another person all one can do is open one's heart to the grace and power of God's love and beg for the grace at least to *want* to forgive. Often, that, in itself, is a miracle of grace and marks the beginning of the process of a new life and a new heart. The simple "Help me, Lord," marks the new life and resurrection that Jesus wants us to share in. We do the impossible in the grace of Jesus as we enter into the mystery of His death and Resurrection where all things are possible.

We also do the impossible, that which we cannot do

by willpower alone, in the community of a Twelve Step Program. What countless numbers of alcoholics and drug addicts could not do alone, they were able to accomplish through the loving support of a group/family/community that challenged and inspired them to new life. What is impossible for us alone becomes possible with God and with one another. It really is not good for us to try to do some things alone. We truly need the loving support of a community to do what is impossible alone.

SECOND SUNDAY OF LENT

Genesis 12:1-4, Psalm 33:4-5, 18-19, 20, 22
2 Timothy 1:8-10
Matthew 17:1-9

"LORD, HOW GOOD IT IS for us to be here." The nervous and frightened words of Peter respond to the dazzling and powerful experience of the Transfiguration. Peter, James and John saw, for the first time, divinity shine through the humanity of their beloved rabbi and friend. I'm sure during dark and difficult moments they thought of that wonderful moment and were strengthened and reassured.

We all need those moments of "transfiguration" when we truly experience the power and presence of God. We need to remember them when things are going badly for us. We need the moments of ecstasy to balance out the moments of agony.

Christians have to be taught to expect the experience of the living God in their prayer life and daily living. We still have so far to go in teaching one another that prayer is not words and formulas. It is not about obligation or duty. It is, rather, putting oneself in the presence of God and being totally open and available for the Lord to communicate with us. All Christians deserve, and will have, their transfiguration experiences if they are prepared and ready to experience the God of passion and power. What is needed is a giant leap beyond the safe prayers that are limited to books and other people's words. We need to propel ourselves into the holy place and it is there that we will find God.

Christians need to discover the Incarnation power in relationships. God *does* come to us in other persons. God is truly present in the loving touch and embrace of husband and wife. Sex is a most powerful vehicle for the communication of the passion and the power of the lover God. Sex can be a true moment of transfiguration as lovers experience the presence and the love of God through the flesh and spirit of spouse.

Our Church has provided many beautiful experiences that can truly be a transfiguration. The Cursillo, Marriage Encounter, Engaged Encounter, Home Retreats, etc., are some of the many ways the Church has found very helpful in creating the atmosphere where the Lord can speak to us and transform our hearts.

Once the Lord touches us, however, once we really experience Him, we can never be the same again. Once we've been to the top of the mountain, we're not content until we climb it again and again. Even if we are dragging ourselves through the dark valley, it helps to know that the mountain is there and we will climb it again.

Monday of the Second Week of Lent
Deuteronomy 9: 4-10, Psalm 79:8, 9, 11, 13
Luke 6: 36-38

YOU CAN ONLY RECEIVE what you have first given to others. Frequently in parish life the community has to deal with great tragedies. Sometimes a tragedy hits someone who is beloved and known for their holiness and charity. So deep and pure is the response that it becomes clear that this is truly a "Jesus moment." The love and compassion is overwhelming and everyone is touched by it.

In reflecting on moments like this, the recipients are always amazed at why people love them so much and why they are so generous to them. They don't have a clue that what they receive is only what they have continually given to others —their love and their heart. Today in the Gospel Jesus tells us that He wants us to be blessed with pardon, compassion, mercy and all material blessings. They can and will be ours if only we first give the same blessings to our dear sisters and brothers.

We do get back what we have first given. As we sow, we also reap. Be extravagant in how you sow. Don't be stingy. The harvest you reap will overwhelm you with its abundance and beauty in this life and the next.

Tuesday of the Second Week of Lent
Isaiah 1:10, 16-20, Psalm 50:8-9, 16-17, 21,23
Matthew 23:1-12

MANY SCRIPTURES make me feel uncomfortable. This one makes me squirm. Imagine if the Lord were saying these terrible things about me or you!

Imagine Him saying that I sit in the chair of Moses and that my people should listen to what I teach, but that they should *not* imitate my example!

Reading on, the picture gets worse: binding up heavy loads and placing them on people's backs, not lifting a finger to help, doing good things only to be seen and praised. Jesus rails against this kind of false religion. But it's so easy to slip into!

Jesus calls us to be a Church of service, a Church of humility and gentleness. It's so easy for the priest, parent, teacher, or for anyone in authority to exercise power rather than humbly serve.

I hate this Gospel; I see too much of myself in it. I see too much of my own tendency to glorify and serve myself and my own agenda. Religion too easily becomes for me a comfortable lifestyle. It's nice to be the king!

It's great to hear the "Yes, Fathers" and "No, Fathers." It's so easy to think you're important, that you're somebody. When I read this Gospel I see too many descriptions of myself that I don't like. How do you feel when you read this

Gospel? Thank God we have another Lent to change the ending of this story. There is hope for us.

Wednesday of the Second Week of Lent
Jeremiah 18:18-20, Psalm 31:5-6, 14, 15-16
Matthew 20:17-28

YOU CAN'T BLAME Mrs. Zebedee. She was only doing what any good parent would do: looking out for her children. While you can't fault mama, you can't be too hard on the boys, either! One might say that they should have known better, but do we know any better two thousand years later? Do we have a clue as to what Jesus expects from those who have authority? We are only beginning to understand.

In the mind of Mrs. Zebedee and her boys, Jesus is going to be a winner. He is going to be a huge success, so why shouldn't the boys cash in on it all? After all, where would Jesus (as nice a man as He is) have gotten without her sons?

"Do you know what you're asking for?" They all say: "Yes," but of course, they have no idea what following Jesus is really all about. Jesus disappoints and disillusions them all. He tells them what discipleship really means: not power and prestige, but the cross and service.

This Lent as we renew our desire to follow Jesus, we are reminded of the cost of discipleship. We have to be willing to lay down our lives in loving service. That's what marriage, priesthood, religious life, single life and friendship all have in common. We must be willing to die for the ones we love. In death we will find our life. How alive are we? Maybe it's necessary to do a little bit more dying before we can truly live. There are parts of our hearts that are not yet redeemed. They must be nailed to the cross this Lent. Only when that is done can we know the new life of Resurrection.

Thursday of the Second Week of Lent
Jeremiah 17:5-10, Psalm 1:1-2, 3, 4, 6
Luke 16:19-31

THE POOR RICH MAN in torment is convinced that if someone should rise from the dead and go back to his brothers, then they would believe and change their lives. Abraham ends the conversation by telling the now poor rich man that if his brothers don't listen to Moses and the prophets, they won't listen even if someone were to come back to them from the dead.

There is always the desire for the novel and the extraordinary in Christianity. People will run all over the world to see apparitions and fail to see the presence of God in their ordinary, day-to-day life. Sometimes that life is downright boring, or maybe we've been so dulled and oppressed that we become boring.

Where is our God? He is within us. He dwells in the people we are with each day. He is found in the daily and sometimes boring things that we do each day. Lent is such a special opportunity to put the spark back into our daily lives. It is a time to find meaning and passion again in what might have become boring and routine. Lent is the time to look at our lives with new eyes, the eyes of faith and love. It is the invitation to love with new fervor and to look at the world and our life and schedules as our daily prayer. *Everything* we do as a Christian is meant to be a prayer. The few moments—like now—when we are formally praying, reading and reflecting help us to look at our lives in a new way.

Our prayer will help us to appreciate the beauty of our lives. We will understand better that our lives are truly holy. When we live them in faith everything becomes an experience of God.

Friday of the Second Week of Lent
Genesis 37:3-4, 12-13, 17-28, Psalm 105:16-21
Matthew 21:33-43, 45-46

TODAY'S GOSPEL forces us to look toward the conclusion of Lent—Holy Week and the Lord's death. As the Church presents us with this painful and somber scene of the son who is murdered, she forces us to consider the reality of our own martyrdom and our own destiny. Martyrdom is part of our life as a Christian.

That martyrdom may indeed be the brutal taking of life as we have seen in the lives of Oscar Romero and the Church Women and Jesuits of El Salvador. Literally, thousands have been called to lay down their lives for what they believe.

Lent is the time when the believer is faced with the reality that to be a Christian is to freely lay down and give one's life. It is not taken away from us, rather we freely give our lives.

As Jesus calls His disciples to love one another as He first loved us, He calls us to love by giving who we are and what we are to our beloved. Our beloved is the Lord, but our beloved is also our spouse, child, friend, parent or parishioner. The gift that we give is the miracle of living for someone else and knowing that love will lead us from death to new life. In that death we nail to the cross all the false gods and idols to which we still cling. As we become free we are able to give the gift of our love. In that giving of our self the Resurrection becomes real in our lives.

Our martyrdom is our voluntary entrance into the mystery of Jesus dying and rising to new life.

Saturday of the Second Week of Lent
Micah 7:14-15, 18-20, Psalm 103:1-2, 3-4, 9-10, 11-12
Luke 15:1-3, 11-32

"This man eats with sinners!" Jesus could have gone far if he had been more careful about the company he kept. Jesus scandalized the establishment of His day by seeking out, welcoming and eating with sinners. This ritual of eating was the way Jesus communicated His love to those who were despised and ostracized from polite society.

This table fellowship of Jesus anticipated the table of the Eucharist. The poor, the sick, prostitutes, tax collectors and the ritual sinners all felt so comfortable breaking bread with Jesus. The same people—you and I—still gather with Him for the breaking of the bread.

The great equalizing factor about Holy Communion is that no one is worthy to be there. We are all sinners. We are all unworthy. A loving God calls us. He welcomes us. He breaks bread with us and He invites us to be bread for one another.

This bread is no reward for a virtuous life. This bread is meant primarily to be the food of sinners. It is meant to give hope and strength to all who eat it. It is meant to console, to heal and to forgive. The Eucharist is the first sacrament of forgiveness in the life of the Church. "Say but the word and my soul shall be healed." "O Lord, I am not worthy!"

Please, never waste your time or energy thinking about, or worse, talking about who should or should not receive Holy Communion. Leave that to the Lord and just fall on your knees and pray over and over again: "I am not worthy! Thank you, Jesus!"

THIRD SUNDAY OF LENT

Exodus 17:3-7, Romans 5:1-2, 5-8
John 4: 5-42

TODAY AS WE READ the Gospel at Mass we are privileged to eavesdrop on the conversation between Jesus and the Samaritan woman. We realize that it is actually Jesus and ourselves in conversation. At the heart of this dialogue Jesus is calling the woman at the well to a new and greater reality. As Jesus requests a drink of water, He is actually inviting her to reflect on the meaning of her life and inviting her to consider something greater than she had ever thought of before. Jesus offers her water with the promise that she will never be thirsty again. Quickly Jesus disposes of concepts like buckets and physical thirst to tell her that what He will give her for the asking is life, eternal life, that can never be taken from her. As Jesus tells her the story of her life, she asks Him to give her this water. She truly thirsts for the living water of God's love.

We are just like the Samaritan woman. We are thirsting for more than the world can give us. Only the thirsty person will look for the source of living water. This Lent Jesus leads us to Himself, the source of all life. The thirsts of our lives make us ready to drink deeply of this water that will truly satisfy. Jesus calls us and invites us to come to Him, the Living Water. The beautiful words of Isaiah remind us that even in our sin and brokenness, even with our failures and broken promises, He loves us and calls us. "You who are thirsty come to the water and drink" *(Isaiah 55:1).*

Monday of the Third Week of Lent
2 Kings 5:1-15, Psalms 42:2-3; 43:3-4
Luke 4:24-30

IT SADDENS JESUS that He is not accepted in His home town of Nazareth. At the heart of His townsfolk's inability to believe in Him is probably that terrible sense of inferiority and disbelief that one of them could ever be good enough to be the prophet. Their own self-hate is projected on Jesus. "How could someone we know be so special?" they think.

Humanity shares this same problem in believing in the Incarnation. How could the Son of God be my brother? How could He be the very flesh of my flesh and bone of my bone? How could I be good enough to say that God *belongs* to me in Christ Jesus?

So many of our problems in accepting the love of God stem from our inability to believe in our own goodness. We cannot accept the fact that God loves us so much that He gives us His only begotten Son to be our Savior and Friend.

It is very hard to believe that the Lord is seeking an intimate relationship with me when I don't believe that I am good enough for Him to want to be my friend. So much of what Lent is about is believing the Good News that He loves me so much and that He wants to be in communion with me. Maybe the more I accept myself, the more I'll be able to accept Him.

Tuesday of the Third Week of Lent
Daniel 3:25, 34-43, Psalm 25:4-5, 6-7, 8-9
Matthew 18: 21-35

When Peter offers his response about how often we must forgive, Jesus multiplies it seventy times to seventy times seven. Peter is totally confused. Isn't that asking for the impossible? The answer is: "Yes!" What Jesus calls for *is* impossible. We cannot do it by ourselves or by our own power.

When Jesus calls Peter and us to this new way of life what He is really calling us to is what He was offering the Samaritan woman on Sunday—a new way of living based on a new life in the Holy Spirit. We *cannot* live the life of Jesus on willpower alone. We *cannot* forgive the way Jesus forgives on willpower alone. Living this way can only come when we've opened up our hearts to the coming of the Holy Spirit.

As we seek such conversion during Lent we are really trying to turn our lives over totally to God and we are begging the Lord to fill us with His Spirit so that we can think and feel and judge with the heart of Jesus. The gift of forgiveness is only part of the treasure of gifts the Holy Spirit will give to us in the new life of Christ. Pray fervently that the Lord will baptize you in His Holy Spirit. Pray that the Spirit will fill you with all of God's gifts, especially forgiveness.

Wednesday of the Third Week of Lent
Deuteronomy 4:1, 5-9, Psalm 147:12-13, 15-16, 19-20
Matthew 5:17-19

Jesus never comes to destroy, neither the law nor the prophets nor us. Jesus transformed and brought to perfect completion the Old Testament and the tradition of Israel. He did *not* discard it or throw it away. That is why we are all Jews. The tradition of Israel lives in us, our faith, Scripture and liturgy. Israel is at the very heart of the Church.

So it is with us in our process of transformation and conversion. As we become a new person in the Holy Spirit, the Lord does not destroy the old man/woman, but rather brings us to perfection. All the qualities and energies in our old life that are not redeemed are now directed in a new and life-giving way.

Lust is a good example. The unredeemed power of lust is completely centered on the self. In redemption, the power matures and seeks the other and becomes love. The redeemed person is still the old person, but also a new and exciting person in whom Christ lives and has freedom to change what is negative into life and resurrection.

In our lifetime the struggle to become the new person never ceases. As long as we are living the Paschal Mystery, Christ's victory is assured and we will know the Resurrection.

Thursday of the Third Week of Lent
Jeremiah 7:23-28, Psalm 95:1-2, 6-7, 8-9
Luke 11:14-23

AM I REALLY *with* Christ or *against* Him? I know that I go through all the forms of seeming to be on His side, but sometimes I'm not sure. It's tempting to take the easy way out of a situation. It's easy to walk a path in which I don't sin seriously, but sometimes that sure and safe way just keeps me comfortable and mediocre. I guess many of our lives are like that—safe.

How boring it is always to be safe and predictable instead of excessive and impulsive. Doesn't it shake you up a bit when you meet somebody who is excessively generous, friendly or helpful? Those are the people who always go the extra mile. They always extend themselves and they always go out of their way for you. They are *clearly* on Christ's side. There is a real passion in their lives so it's exciting to be with them. They inspire you to be more than you are. They encourage you not to live by minimalism even if it's the letter of the law and you're *technically* OK.

Every so often someone like St. Francis, Mother Theresa or Pope John comes along and teaches us by their example what it really means to be on His side. Let's face it—if we're not clearly on the Lord's side then we're really not with Him. We're playing it safe. We're lukewarm and we're in danger of being spit out of His mouth. Don't be afraid. Take the leap and really be on His side.

Friday of the Third Week of Lent
Hosea 14:2-10; Psalm 81:6-8, 8-9, 10-11, 14,17
Mark 12:28-34

TO LOVE with all you've got! That's what He wants and that's all that makes sense. Powerful, passionate and total love is all that is fitting for the Lord God. A weak, inconsistent, fickle, changeable love is not worthy of Him. It's a sham unworthy of the King of Kings. Christianity is the school of love. Everything the Church does is meant to teach us how to love—to love with all our hearts and souls and minds and strength.

Christianity can never be a spectator sport. We can't just admire the Lord from a distance. We're called to be totally involved with Him. We're expected to give Him everything we've got—to hold back nothing. We have to love Him passionately until we're breathless. When we love Him like that we pick up the Scriptures and the words jump out at us because they are so filled with His power and beauty. When we love this way our hearts are burning within us as we receive the Holy Eucharist. When we love Him like this we become better lovers to everyone in our lives. This love of God so touches us that we become capable of loving our spouse, our children and our friends more than we were able to without totally loving God.

To love God this way is to set the world on fire. There

is no way to put that fire out once it starts. Don't be afraid to love Him. Once you do, you'll really know what it is to be alive.

Saturday of the Third Week of Lent
Hosea 6:1-6; Psalm 51:3-4, 18-19, 20-21
Luke 18:9-14

"O GOD, be merciful to me, a sinner." This prayer of the sinner is the prayer of the real saint. The closer one comes to God the more one becomes aware of one's sinfulness. The holy person makes the most sincere and beautiful confession. The holy person weeps for his/her sins and never has a problem numbering and confessing them.

The person far away from God does much better confessing other people's sins. He/she becomes an expert at putting blame and guilt on other people. It is *always* someone else's fault or sin. The sinner is always judging other people but never using the same measure to judge him/herself.

What a blessing it is to know your sins and to bring them to the Lord. At this time it's good to think about our Lenten Confession. How do I love my God, my wife, my husband, my children, my friends, etc.? Do I love them the way Jesus loved—to the point of laying down His life for His beloved?

You will find so much to confess, not because you're evil, but because you're good and you have grown in sensitivity to the beauty and holiness of the God of love. With all your heart you will pray the beautiful and humble words of our tax collector friend: *"O God, be merciful to me, a sinner!"*

THE FOURTH SUNDAY OF LENT
1 Samuel 16:1, 6-7, 10-13, Psalm 23:1-3, 3-4, 5, 6
Ephesians 58-14
John 9:1-41

OF ALL THE AFFLICTIONS a person can have, blindness always seems to me to be the worst. Imagine being unable to see the beauty around you—the face of your child, a flower.

The man born blind literally walks into his salvation as he encounters the Son of God and the process of gaining his sight begins. It is interesting that what we see here is not the curing of the blindness, but rather the process of regaining sight.

Lent is supposed to be like that for us. We possess everything. We have everything, but we don't fully see it or appreciate it. What the Lord does for us in this holy time is to take the blindness away so that we begin to see what has always been there.

We are invited to "see" the love of God and His call to new life. We are invited to "see" the holiness that is already in our lives as we rediscover our marriage, parenthood, priesthood, friendship, etc. Our spirituality consists in appreciating and claiming the holy that is already in all that we possess and all that we do. There is nothing new that the Lord can give us—we already have it all. We already possess everything.

In this time of Lent we pray for the grace to be healed of our blindness so that we can begin to see what we already have and appreciate it and know it for the first time.

Monday of the Fourth Week of Lent
Isaiah 65:17-21, Psalm 30:2, 4, 5-6, 11-13
John 4:43-54

IN TODAY'S GOSPEL Jesus comes in contact with faith and love on the part of a non-believer, the royal official. The official is struggling to believe in Jesus. It's a healthy thing for us to reflect about how much we struggle with our faith. By faith, I don't just mean accepting the tenets of the Creed. We do that because it has very little impact on the way we live. It really doesn't make much difference in our practical lives if there are three or ten persons in God. Real faith means totally trusting and placing our lives in God's hands. That's what the official is being asked to do. We are being led to the point of handing over to the Lord everything we possess and believing that the Lord will provide for us and take care of us.

We all struggle with that as the official did. He had a very hard time handing over his son to Jesus. We all have areas in our lives that we hold on to and don't trust Jesus with. There are things we're afraid to give up and give over to Jesus. The prayer of this official who is struggling to say *"yes"* to Jesus will help us in our journey toward conversion this Lent. What we are being called to is to say our total *"yes"* to Jesus.

Tuesday of the Fourth Week of Lent
Ezekiel 47:1-9,12, Psalm 46:2-3, 5-6, 8-9
John 5:1-3, 5-16

IMAGINE BEING SICK for thirty-eight years! Imagine caring for someone for that time! Yet, that is the life of many people who bear physical and emotional pain day in and day out for years. Our little penances during Lent should help to bring us closer to the part of the Body of Christ that is in pain.

Notice what Jesus does when He cures this sick man. He gives him a job: *"Pick up your mat and walk."* All too often we miss the point of our own healings. Jesus doesn't forgive us or heal us just to make us feel better. Rather, when He heals us He gives us a job. The job is always to give away the gift He's given to us to someone who needs it.

For example when Jesus gives the gift of sobriety to the alcoholic, He expects that person to help bring someone else to sobriety. When Jesus forgives *us*, He expects us to give forgiveness to someone who has hurt us.

Jesus expects us not only to accept our healing but also to live as a healed and happy person. We cannot just lie there when we've been healed. We have to get up, pick up our mat and begin to walk. When we do so we begin to give healing to someone else.

Wednesday of the Fourth Week of Lent
Isaiah 49:8-15, Psalm 145:8-9, 13-14, 17-18
John 5:17-30

THE READING from Isaiah today has a definite Advent ring to it. It is a message of hope and consolation to the downtrodden and alienated. It is a call for justice and freedom for all as we share with each other the gift of love that He first gives to us.

Isaiah touches the universal pain of the human family. That pain has been experienced so profoundly in our own day. People cry out as they did in Isaiah's day: "Does God exist?" "Does He *really* care about me?" "How can He allow the evil that goes on in the world?"

God's answer is found at the end of this passage in the most touching and beautiful words of all Scripture: *"Can a mother forget her infant, be without tenderness for the child in her womb? Even so, I will never forget you."* We are reminded today that God is our Mother loving us with the total, fierce and all consuming love of a mother for her child. That love is the most powerful force in all the world. Our greatest challenge in Lent will be to accept that gift of love that our Mother God is offering to us without price or condition. It is ours for the taking.

Thursday of the Fourth Week of Lent
Exodus 32:7-14, Psalm 106:19-20, 21-22, 23
John 5:31-47

IN THE READING from Exodus today we have the exciting scene of Moses coming down from Mount Sinai with the Ten Commandments ready to give the Israelites hell for making and worshipping a graven image—the golden calf. Cecil B. DeMille created a scene that we're not likely ever to forget. The whole scene seems so primitive and unsophisticated. Imagine, a golden calf that people bend their knees before.

But is it really so far-fetched? Idolatry is *still* the prime sin of society. We have become classier in our idolatries, it's true. Instead of the molten golden calf, we choose idols that are called by other names like power, success, prestige, control, self-righteousness, religion, lust and materialism. Oh, it's true we don't dance around these idols and bend our knees before them. All we do is devote our whole lives to them while we neglect the one true God of love who *cannot* and *will not* share center stage with any lesser gods.

Since Lent began have we at least identified the gods we worship, and begun the difficult process of turning them into dust just like Moses did at the Mountain of Sinai?

There is only *one* God. Do you worship Him or another?

Friday of the Fourth Week of Lent
Wisdom 2:1, 12-22, Psalm 34:17-18, 19-20, 21, 23
John 7:1-2,10, 25-30

IN THE READING from Wisdom today we have a different "feel" for Isaiah's suffering Servant. We are beginning to see and feel the shadow of the cross and we are not too happy about it. We really don't want the cross. We ignore it, deny it and often act as if it were not an essential or necessary part of Christianity, but it is. There's no getting away from it.

The cross is at the very center of the redemptive act of Jesus. He chooses to lay down His life in ransom for ours. He holds back nothing, giving everything—to the last drop of His Blood—that we might be saved. On the cross, Jesus embraces humanity completely as He shares in the agony and pain of every person who has ever lived. We have a Savior Who has lived every aspect of life—beautiful and horrible—and He is with us as we live the cross now.

Jesus on the cross identifies and becomes one with all those who are crucified by our society today. He shares in the poverty of the homeless; He suffers with those dying of AIDS. He is despised along with the homosexuals. He is ignored with the Blacks and Hispanics. He is the humble, broken servant calling us to share in the pain He endures today in His sisters and brothers. He calls us to work for justice for all people because there is no true faith and no true religion without justice and respect for all people.

Saturday of the Fourth Week of Lent
Jeremiah 11:18-20, Psalm 7:2-3, 9-10, 11-12
John 7:40-53

IN THE GOSPEL today a great deal is made of this "lot" who believe in Jesus. They are dismissed by the religious as knowing nothing about the law and as being people who are lost anyway because of their "sinfulness" and "ignorance."

Isn't it humbling how the "sinners" often turn out to be much holier than the religious? And how the "religious" delight in deciding who is not "in" or "saved" or "allowed" to go to Communion? The truly religious people condemn no one, because they know they are guilty of things they might condemn in someone else, or if they're not, it's only God's grace that has preserved them. The truly religious people always *include,* they never *exclude.* They are deeply concerned about the salvation of everyone, but never take it upon themselves to judge others. They leave that up to God. They hate sin but love the sinner. They weep for the pain of someone who has sinned, but they avoid giving lectures. They just love, and they are there when a sister or brother needs them.

These holy people see good where others are able to see only evil. They heal, they console, they forgive, and they challenge with a gentle and loving touch. When they touch you, you know that Jesus touches you.

THE FIFTH SUNDAY OF LENT

Ezekiel 37:12-14, Psalm 130:1-2, 3-4, 5-6, 7-8, Romans 8:8-11
John 11:1-45

"AND JESUS BEGAN TO WEEP." These words from today's Gospel are the most beautiful statement of the meaning of the Incarnation for me. Jesus is not pretending. He feels with all His being the pain, terror, confusion and anger that is appropriate at the death of a beloved friend. Jesus is really one of us. He is not an actor, well-schooled at this thing called humanity. He is not acting. No, He's ours. He belongs to us. He is our brother. Jesus at Lazarus' tomb doesn't offer up pious platitudes like: "It's God's will—he's in a better place." Jesus does the only thing He has any right to do as a human being—He weeps. There are no words to say when someone is broken-hearted—all you can do is be there and share the pain. Jesus shares the pain of loss with Martha and Mary.

It's so hard to lose someone you love dearly. I have celebrated hundreds of funerals. Some of them are very matter-of-fact. There seems to be very little feeling or emotion on the part of the mourners. Others are very moving and holy experiences. The deceased is obviously deeply loved by the mourners. The death of this beloved person will touch and influence the lives of his/her family and friends for years to come. Life will never be quite the same for them. Their tears are so sincere, and so beautiful and holy.

How blest these people are to love someone so much! How fortunate they are to have lived the very heart of humanity—love and relationship. The Church will lead these holy people through their tears to the mystery of Resurrection. She will pose the question of Jesus to Martha: "Do you believe? Do you believe that I conquer even death and that your brother will live forever and that you will all be together again in the Kingdom?"

With Mary, these broken-hearted people—you and me—will respond: "Yes." But even in our most sincere "yes," the pain can be intolerable. We pray with Thomas: *"Lord, I believe, but help my unbelief!"*

Monday of the Fifth Week of Lent
Deuteronomy 13:1-9, 15-17, 19-30, 33-62,
Psalm 23:1-3, 3-4, 5, 6
John 8:12-20

JESUS CHANGES the life of Mary Magdalene, who has been caught in adultery, by simply respecting her and loving her. Perhaps He's one of the first men to ever look at Mary without lust. Jesus sees in her not sin, but a beautiful person who has been hurt and abused over the years, perhaps beginning with her own father. She now believes that she's worth nothing and that she has no value. Prostitution of all kinds is the normal conclusion to a life lacking in love and affirmation.

What is Jesus writing in the sand after He tells the men that the one without sin should cast the first stone? Jesus is probably writing in the sand the sins of those gathered around holding the biggest stones. They just can't wait to let her have it! They are so filled with the holy righteousness of God. Ha! Their false anger veils their own lust.

One by one they drop their stones and walk away, leaving Jesus and Mary alone. *"Does no one condemn you? Neither do I. Go now, and avoid this sin."*

Did Mary never sin again? We don't know. This we do know: Mary knew she had a Savior Who loved her and would always forgive her. So do we.

When we have learned personally the meaning of forgiveness we will be very slow to condemn anyone.

Tuesday of the Fifth Week of Lent
Numbers 21:4-9, Psalm 102:2-3, 16-18, 19-21
John 8:21-30

TODAY JESUS refers to His crucifixion when He speaks about being lifted up. It is in looking upon Christ crucified that we come to understand who He really is and what He is about. Jesus is the eternal Word of the Father who takes flesh and blood to remind us forever of the Father's love.

In these days of Lent our prayer should be centered on the cross and mystery of God's Love. The Father gives us His beloved Son *(John 3:16)*. So great is His love that He gives us His Beloved and Precious One—the Word. The Father holds nothing back. His Son becomes our Brother. He belongs to us as He does to the Father. He is flesh of our flesh and bone of our bone.

Freely the Son embraces the cross. His death is the most complete and total "I love you!" that has ever been spoken. He gives us everything, even to the last drop of His Blood, so that we might have a new life.

He speaks to us from the cross and reminds us to love one another as He has first loved us. He reminds us to lay down our lives each day in love for one another. He tells us to hold back nothing. Only then will we come to know who we truly are. If we ever question His love, we only have to look at the cross to see how much He loved us.

Wednesday of the Fifth Week of Lent
Daniel 3:14-20, Daniel 3:52, 53, 54, 55, 56
John 8: 31-42

JESUS TELLS US today to live in the truth. The truth/light theme is found all through John. Those who walk with Jesus live in the truth. They are transparent. They fear nothing and they hide nothing. The liar and the thief live in constant fear of the truth and the light. They are always afraid of being discovered and found out. They have no peace and no real security.

Lent is the time to rededicate ourselves to the truth and to walk in the light. We want to avoid any hint of living double lives or having double standards. We always want to be committed to the truth of what is right.

When we stand for the truth we also stand for justice for all people. We become passionate for the rights of other people. We cannot be at peace when another person is suffering from prejudice or injustice. We work for justice and the rights of all. Passion for the truth has that effect on us!

As we stand by the cross, the light of the Lord's love dispels all shadows and we stand in the brightness of His truth. We never have anything to fear or hide when we live in His truth.

Thursday of the Fifth Week of Lent
Genesis 17:3-9, Psalm 105:4-5, 6-7, 8-9
John 8:51-59

THE FIRST READING from Genesis today speaks of the covenant Passover between Abram and Yahweh. Yahweh promises Abram that he will be the father of nations. Yahweh would always be faithful to this covenant even when Israel was unfaithful. This covenant is often described in terms of a marriage relationship as Yahweh courts and woos his beloved spouse. He calls her back into the desert to renew the bond of love after Israel's infidelity.

During Lent we prepare to renew our marriage covenant with our God as we prepare to renew the Promises of Baptism at Easter Mass. The Lord has led us into the desert of Lent that He might speak to our hearts as He invites us to fall in love again with Him and renew the love of our youth. The desert is like the second honeymoon time in which the Lord invites us into a deepened relationship with Him.

We celebrate a love in which the Lord has forgiven us and restored us to a place of honor as He reminds us of His unending and powerful love which will never come to an end. The Lord invites us simply to accept that gift of His love.

Even if we have neglected our relationship with the Lord, there is a new and beautiful opportunity this Lent to renew it.

Friday of the Fifth Week of Lent
Jeremiah 20:10-13, Psalm 18:2-3, 3-4, 5-6, 7
John 10:31-42

IN THE GOSPEL today Jesus calls for faith on the part of the people because He is doing the works of His Father. He calls them to believe in His works even if they can't believe in Him.

What do people see about your work? Is it obvious to everyone the person for whom you are really working? Is it clear that your life and labor flow from a deep faith in Our Lord Jesus Christ?

Ministerial work should obviously be an extension of our faith in the Lord. It should be very clear as we perform our ministries that Jesus is the author. Yet, the works can become ends in themselves. Often they can be performed in a secular way without real love and vision of the Lord. Sometimes, the Church can do very unchristian things in the name of Jesus. Sometimes, Church people are too much into status and power, and they forget that the meaning of ministry is service and humility.

Our secular work must also reflect the presence of the Lord. What beautiful works of evangelization, healing and mercy the Christian is able to do at work! The man or woman who is tolerant, kind, just and polite will cause people to ask a question: "Why is he/she like that?" The answer is Jesus!

Saturday of the Fifth Week of Lent
Ezekiel 37:21-28; Jeremiah 31:10, 11-12, 13
John 11:45-57

JESUS IS A SIGN of contradiction. In today's Gospel some people, who visited Mary after Jesus raised Lazarus, put their faith in Him; others plotted to kill Him.

What does Jesus do to the people? Jesus is someone people deeply admire. The Gospels present a beautiful way of life that makes a lot of sense and shows a way of life that is richly blessed. All through the ages Jesus has touched the minds and hearts of countless people who have been touched by His word.

But Jesus calls us to follow Him, not just to admire Him. He enters our lives and says: *"Come, follow Me!"* The call to be a disciple of Jesus is actually an invitation to share His life in a very personal and intimate way.

In my spiritual life it is not enough to know *about* Him, I must *know* Him. I must have *His* mind and heart as my mind and heart. Following Jesus as His disciples means giving Him everything and holding on to nothing. The paradox of the Paschal Mystery is that as I give Him everything I actually gain everything.

As I enter this mystery of His death and resurrection I give away everything and I gain more. In losing my life I actually find my life.

It is so hard to take the plunge and jump into His arms! We are all so afraid that He will want too much. Until we take the plunge we will never know what life is all about and what we can possess as we lose everything.

Don't be afraid. Take the plunge.

HOLY WEEK~PALM SUNDAY
Matthew 21:1-11 or Mark 11:1-10 or John 12:12-16
Isaiah 50:4-7, Psalm 22, Philippians 2:6-11
Passion Accounts:
Matthew 27:11-54, Mark 15:1-39, Luke 23:1-49

PALM SUNDAY is one of the really great days in parish life. Something wonderful happens as the church is packed with people clutching their precious palms, priests in red vestments, the altar and sanctuary decorated festively, acknowledging that Jesus is our King. Palm Sunday is a true community celebration. There is a joy that seems to fill everyone's heart as we remember once again how much He loves us.

The reading of the Passion is an invitation to listen with the heart to the greatest love story that has ever been told. My God has loved me so much that He gave me His only Son to be my brother and my friend. This Jesus completes the story by freely laying down His life on the cross for me. My name is written in the heart of Jesus as He dies on the cross so that I might live.

On Palm Sunday we remember the times that we have shouted: "Hosanna!" We also remember the times that we have shouted: "Crucify Him!" We remember our fidelity and our infidelity. We celebrate the fact that our Lord prefers to forgive us rather than condemn us. He clothes us in the white garment of his love and peace. This holy day is such a wonderful time to remember that even when we were sinners He loved us and He forgave us.

As I place my palm in my room there will be many times in the coming year when I will glance at it. When I do, I will remember that on Palm Sunday I declared that Jesus Christ was my King.

Monday of Holy Week
Isaiah 42:1-7, Psalm 27:1, 2, 3, 13-14
John 12: 1-11

THERE HE GOES AGAIN! Another party, another banquet and Jesus at the head of the table being honored! Lazarus is near Jesus. Mary is there and the apostles are guests. Martha is serving–of course!

During the meal Mary does something that is completely extravagant but deeply moving. She anoints the feet of Jesus with the precious ointment and dries them with her hair. Judas speaks on behalf of everyone there: "What a waste." Indeed, everyone in that room thought it was a waste, everyone except Jesus. The fragrance of the perfume filled that whole house for a long time.

"What a waste!" These words are often used to describe a young man or woman choosing to serve the Body of Christ in poverty, chastity and obedience. They are used to describe a teacher, a social worker or an attorney opting to work for the poor. "What a waste," as Christians depart to work with the poorest of the poor in foreign missions.

Thank God there are so many beautifully simple and humble disciples who choose to serve the Lord and the Body of Christ by "wasting" their time, talent and treasures on the least of Jesus' sisters and brothers.

When they do so, the House of the Lord—this world—is filled with the fragrance of love and generosity that remains and influences us for generations to come, just like the wasted perfume poured on the feet of Jesus.

Tuesday of Holy Week
Isaiah 49:1-6, Psalm 71:1-2, 3-4, 5-6, 17
John 13:21-33, 36-38

MAKE NO MISTAKE about it: Judas is in heaven. The loving Jesus who called Judas and who loved him so much would not, could not, allow him to be lost. Jesus loved Judas in such a special way. He called him to be one of the foundation stones of His Church. He would never let him get away.

God pursues us. He never lets us get away from Him. He truly is the Hound of Heaven as Francis Thompson portrays Him. Think of how God pursued Judas and Francis. Think of how God has pursued you all through your life. You made choices that were not the best, but He used them as a way of your finding Him. He even has taken your sins and failures and turned them around and made them sources of grace.

God's love will not be thwarted. It is so humbling to know that God is so hopelessly in love with us that He will never let us get away; that He will pursue us through "labyrinthine ways" until He finds us and we open our hearts to Him and say: "Yes!"

This Holy Week forces us to look at the cross of Jesus. It forces us to see this love that is so personal and so complete. It embarrasses and it challenges us. Why do we resist Him so much? No matter how long it takes, His love will conquer all.

Saint Judas, pray for us!

Wednesday of Holy Week
Isaiah 50:4-9, Psalm 69:8-10, 21-22, 31, 33-34
Matthew 26:14-25

JUDAS IS TRAPPED. He can't get out of this. In the musical *Godspell* the torture of Judas was powerfully portrayed as he leaves the Last Supper and pushes against the air in all directions as if he were a trapped animal in a cage—and so he was.

This sad night—Spy Wednesday, as it used to be called—reminds me of so many people who are trapped in situations, circumstances and relationships they can't get out of.

We preach that salvation and freedom are possible for everyone, but that's not completely true. There are people who have made choices that have created situations that they are incapable of changing. They live in a veritable hell for years and years. For some, death will be the only way out.

Many of us commit "easy" sins. We go to confession and the slate is clean and we begin again. Others commit "stupid" sins in which they, in effect, sell their souls to the devil and pay for it for the rest of their lives. Just because you and I were lucky does not mean that we are better than those sisters and brothers who would love to be able to start again, but cannot. Be very slow in ever judging anyone and remember—that except for the grace of God there go you, Judas.

Pray tonight for those you know and don't know who have been trapped by their poor choices and circumstances and are yearning for the redemption and peace that you and I take for granted. St. Judas, pray for them!

THE GREAT THREE DAYS
Holy Thursday~The Lord's Supper

Exodus 12:1-8, 11-14, Psalm 116:12-13, 15-16, 17-18,
1 Corinthians 11:23-26
John 13:1-15

THERE IS A MOMENT in the Liturgy of the Mass of the Lord's Last Supper that seems to transcend time and space. It occurs when I remove my chasuble, pour water in a basin, wrap a towel around myself as an apron and begin to wash the feet of my dear parishioners, my dear family, my sisters and brothers—the Body of Christ.

At that blessed moment as I go from apostle to apostle, the Church reminds me what my priesthood is all about. I am called to serve His people, not to be served. I am called to lay down my life in loving service for my dear family.

Once Jesus, the good Rabbi, gave the Apostles His own Body and Blood to be their food and drink. He ordained them, set them apart to serve the community by celebrating the Eucharist until He comes again. To make sure they understood what it would mean to celebrate the Eucharist and to receive the Eucharist, He used an audio-visual aid. He washed their feet.

On Holy Thursday night every Christian is reminded again—powerfully, emotionally and effectively—what it means to be a Eucharistic people. We must be a people who are living the meaning of the Eucharist by our care for one another—especially the poor and the alienated. It also teaches us that if the Eucharist is celebrated without being a pledge of love and service to all, especially the poor, it is empty, meaningless and vain.

At the morning Holy Thursday Mass for our children, our parents are invited to come forth and wash the feet of their beloved sons and daughters as the clergy assist them.

How powerful it is to see our saints, our holy parents, participate in the washing, the total commitment of love that their parenthood truly is. Their beloved children are the Body of Christ, not only at the Washing, but in the day-in and day-out living of their parenthood. What they do and who they are is holy and precious in God's eyes.

The Church has nothing to give these saints to make them holy. They *are* holy. They *already* possess everything. It will be the Church's great joy on Holy Thursday and on every Sunday to remind them of what they already possess—the love and the holiness of the Lord Jesus. The Church will echo to them the words of Jesus: *"Love one another as I have loved you" (John 15:17).*

Good Friday~The Passion of the Lord
Isaiah 52:13-53, 12, Psalm 31:2, 6, 12-13, 15-16, 17, 25,
Hebrews 4:14-16, 5, 7-9
John 18:1-19:42

AFTER THE READING of the Passion of John and after the sermon, the people of God come two by two to venerate the crucifix. I have a wonderful vantage point at the foot of the cross from which to observe this procession. We use only one crucifix that is life-size. We encourage our people to take their time and to make this their special moment with Jesus. What a moment it is for all of us as the choir leads us in the touching hymns and chants of the day.

I look out and see throngs of people so respectful and so touched by the drama and the prayer that is taking place. The old and the young are there—children, parents and grandparents—those who are always at church, those who are never at church. Some touch the Corpus, others kiss it and others embrace it, while still others just weep and gently bow. Everyone is deeply sensitive that this is a very special moment to tell Jesus how much we love Him. It is also a moment when people weep for their sins at the cross.

The procession is the March of Life. There's the young woman who had an abortion. Lord, please let this be the time for her to believe in Your love and to begin to forgive herself as You already have. There's the couple who seem to have fallen out of love and are struggling desperately to put the pieces together. Jesus, help them to find their love again. There's the homeless man, the poorest of the poor. I know he's the holiest of all of us, but there's no reaching him, he won't let anyone do anything for him. Lord, I'm so sorry for the times that I resent him coming to me. It's always at the worst possible time. Look, he's crying so hard as he kisses Your feet. Forgive me, Jesus. I'm so sorry.

Lord, there's the woman who's going into the hospital on Monday for tests. She's terrified. She's afraid the cancer is back again. She begs You to let her be OK—just for her kids. She doesn't want them to be without a mother.

Jesus, it seems like the end will never come. They keep coming and coming and coming. Your holy people, Your Living Body, Your Church is together at the foot of Your cross, pouring out all its love and faith and begging You to help us in our own personal crucifixions.

Dear Jesus, You continue to be crucified in the agony and pain of Your people. Let each of us know today that we do not suffer alone but that You are always at our side. You are our Savior and our friend.

Holy Saturday~Suffering and Triumph of the Servant of the Lord
Isaiah 52:13-53:12

TODAY IS the great Sabbath rest as we await the Lord's resurrection. In our church the statue of the dead Christ lies in state while confessions are heard. All day long people come to watch and pray at this holy place. Again our people need to touch and kiss the statue. The physical and tangible is so helpful to our prayer and understanding of these holy events. We wait with Jesus with the knowledge that He will rise, and our prayer is a prayer of hope and petition begging the Lord that we might also rise again and leave behind in the tomb all that is dead and decaying, all that stinks.

As we wait with Jesus we wait in hope, sure that new life is ours for the asking and that Easter will mean a new beginning of life and another chance to get it right this time.

In late afternoon many people gather together around the dead Christ to pray midday prayer. It is our last time together before the Easter Vigil and the Eucharists of Easter Day. It is our final moment to prayerfully thank the Lord for the graces of Lent and Holy Week and for the incredible grace of having a family in faith to share the events of salvation. For all the beauty and power of these holy days, what would they all mean without sisters and brothers who not only believe with us but nourish, increase, and at times, challenge our faith?

This holy time is the opportunity for the Church to pass through the paschal mystery. Lent, Holy Week and Easter are not just times for individuals to be changed and healed. These days are also meant for the Church itself to repent of her sins, to beg pardon, to make peace and to confess with all her heart that Jesus is the only Lord and that we, personally, and as His Church, are His unworthy servants in constant need of reformation and purification.

Personally and institutionally we are called to give up power, abusive authority, lack of faith, materialism and mistrust of God's people and to look to Jesus as the Suffering Servant who comes not to be served, but to serve, and to give His life as ransom for many.

"Christ for our sakes became obedient until death, even

death on a Cross, for which God has exalted Him and given Him the name above every other name" (Philippians 2).

The Great Vigil of Easter

*TONIGHT WE HEAR the story of our salvation—the story of God's total love for us from the beginning of time. If you are not able to reflect on all of the readings, I suggest the ones which are highlighted: Genesis 1:1-2:2; Genesis 22:1-18; **Exodus 14:15-15:1**; Isaiah 54:5-14; Isaiah 55:1-11; Baruch 3:9-15, 32-4:4; Ezekiel 36:16-28; **Romans 6:3-11** and **Matthew 28:1-10.***

If there were ever a time when the Church pulls out all the stops, it's tonight! The Great Vigil of Easter is a time for God's people to come together and wait or vigil for the dawn for the Resurrection of the Lord Jesus Christ.

There are moments in our life when we are called upon to share our heart, all that we are, and all that we know, with someone we love. Moments like that occur when we are at the bedside of someone who is very ill. They occur when a son or daughter is leaving home to go to college, to marry, or for a job transfer. They happen when our child has their own child. They are peak moments of communication when we try to say everything that is in our hearts.

The Easter Vigil is one of those moments. The Church tries to tell her new members who will be baptized and those who will renew their Baptism all she can about Jesus, life and salvation. She does this through signs and symbols like light and darkness, fire and smoke, oil and water, the laying on of hands, and bread and wine. All these elements together attempt to explain the mystery of salvation which we experience in Jesus Christ as we die with Him and rise to a new and glorious life.

The Church tries to put the finishing touches on her new members tonight as she calls them to the waters of Baptism; as she pours the Oil of Gladness over them; as she plunges them forth to a new life of Jesus in the Holy Sacrament of the Eucharist.

In many divine and beautiful ways the Church will explain to them what it means to die to sin and to rise to a new life. The Church will teach them that what they believe in—this new life in Jesus—they will actually experience and live in the sacraments of the Body of Christ. The Church will teach them that they will become part of the Body of Christ, so real and so intense will be their identification with Jesus.

As the community sees their new sisters and brothers pass through this mystery of death and life, each of us will renew our own personal death to sin and resurrection to the New Life in Jesus Christ. We will each say our "Yes" again to Jesus, to life, to hope and to one another.

EASTER SUNDAY

Acts 10:34, 37-43, Psalm 118, 1 Corinthians 5:6-8
John 20:1-9

THE WHOLE WORLD rejoices as our churches are packed with believers today—Jesus is risen from the dead. The throngs of people that are present *do* believe. Even if many don't come to church during the year, there is that seed of faith in their hearts waiting for the right moment, right place, right moisture to break into life.

This is true of the people at your church this morning, both the regulars and the visitors.We are all waiting for that moment to break into a new life. Isn't this Easter my special invitation to work on my own personal problems and live the new life with Christ? Isn't it time finally to die to what is old and to rise to the new life which He wants me to have in abundance? Each of us has a history and story. Hasn't it been said that every *saint* has a history and every *sinner* has a chance? Easter is our big chance to put things right and start again.

As Mary comes to the tomb she knows that the stone has to be rolled away. She also knows that she's not able to do it herself. She believes that somehow the Lord will provide and He will take care of it all—and He does!

Mary's attitude should be a great encouragement for us at Easter. We don't have to do it all ourselves. The Lord is there for us. We can't push the stone away from our hearts all by ourselves. That's why we have a Savior. That's why we have Jesus.

Christianity is not the religion of willpower alone. Christianity is the faith that proclaims that when we are weak, it is then that we are strong. Christianity looks to a Savior who will push the stone *with* us, not instead of us.

Resurrection faith is the acknowledgment that Jesus lives and that His life is now our life. The Lord calls us to claim our resurrection with and in Him. The Lord reminds us that He is always with us and that in Him all things are possible.

At Easter the Church proclaims the Gospel of Hope—hope for the world and hope for us personally. At Easter the Church calls humanity to heal the wounds of hate and disunity. The resurrection of Christ from the dead is the promise that life and love will always win out over death and hate. In His resurrection Christ rewrites the Book of Genesis. Creation begins again.

6.

The Via Dolorosa

MOST OF US were brought up with the practice of making the Stations of the Cross on the Fridays of Lent. Could anyone ever forget the melody of the **Stabat Mater**? *"At the Cross her station keeping, close to Jesus to the last."*

In every church the fourteen Stations on the walls invite us to make the journey with Jesus to Calvary. Lent is always a special time to accept that invitation and make the journey with Jesus.

I will never forget a trip I made to the Holy Land several years ago. My group arrived after dark and our hotel was located outside the walls of the old city. After unpacking, my good friend, Fr. Charlie Papa and I decided to go exploring in the old city. We found ourselves making our way along narrow, old, and deserted streets. It was a scary place—especially in the dark and deserted areas.We both happened to look up at the same time and saw a street sign that read: *Statio Tertia—The Third Station*. We realized that this was the traditional spot of the *Third Station—Jesus Falls for the First Time* and that we had been making the Stations without knowing it. We began to pray as we realized the holy ground we were standing on.

In the midst of our prayer we heard snoring in a room above the street. And I mean snoring! We burst into laughter at this angelic choir backing up our prayer. But then it dawned on both of us that most of us snore through the Stations every day because we are unaware that Jesus continues to suffer in the lives of all of our brothers and sisters all over the world. We are all walking the Stations of the cross with Jesus as we become part of the lives of one another and the whole world.

These meditations will not take the traditional form of St. Alphonsus Liguori. His beautiful meditations focus on the historical sufferings of Jesus. They will, rather, flow from more of a liberation theology and spirituality in trying to see the sufferings of Christ as they are being lived out today in the lives of men, women and children all over the world. They will at times make us feel guilty because they will confront us with the challenge that being a Christian is more than ethical living. Christianity is also a commitment to see and minister to Jesus in all people, especially the poorest of the poor.

Remember—our prayer is not just a nostalgic visit to the past, but to what those terrible events say to us in our daily struggle as we make a living, raise our children and live the Gospel in this day and age.

Jesus Christ did suffer and die two thousand years ago. Through those sufferings, resurrection and new life came into the world. But Jesus Christ continues to suffer and die in the poor. The mandate of His Church is to transform the world and bring resurrection to His contemporary suffering and death.

With that in mind let us walk with Jesus along the Via Dolorosa.

First Station
Jesus Is Condemned to Death

We adore Thee O Christ and we bless Thee
because by Thy Holy Cross Thou hast redeemed the world.

THERE ARE so many people in our world condemned to

death. The people condemned to death by courts and tribunals just as Jesus was come to mind first. They are the minority.

We live in a world where Jesus is condemned to death not just by the death penalty but by the moral climate of a world where the human person has become expendable.

We think of the thousands of human persons destroyed each day in the holocaust of abortions. War claims its deadly toll each and every day especially in the third world countries who pay top dollar for instruments of death from the affluent and powerful nations like the United States and Britain. So many poor countries prefer to buy the toys of the "big boys" rather than to buy food for their starving children. Jesus is condemned to death through the horrors of war and aggression each day.

Millions of land mines continue to maim and kill thousands each year including innocent children at play and farmers who work the soil. Jesus is condemned as our own country leads the list of the providers of these obscene instruments of death and torture.

Jesus is condemned to death in the countries of the world where ethnic cleansing is still the number one sport of the military. Rape, murder and torture seem to be real fun to many governments who delight in dismembering and destroying "the other." Even *alleged* Christian leaders join in the fun while they attend the Stations of the Cross during Lent in their parish churches!

Jesus is condemned to death in our cities where poverty is still allowed to reign and poor children have inadequate housing, nutrition and education. They live in terrible worlds where it is so easy to be a slave of drugs and crime.

And Jesus is condemned when we don't listen and turn off other people because they are different or don't agree with us. In this season of hope, the Lord invites us to give life and hope to one another, not death and despair.

Second Station
Jesus Carries His Cross

We adore Thee O Christ and we bless Thee
because by Thy Holy Cross Thou hast redeemed the world.

JESUS EMBRACES his cross and begins to carry it to Calvary. Make no mistake about it, we all must carry our cross. How we carry it will determine our happiness and peace in this life and will be our promise of eternal life.

Usually when presented with the cross our first reaction is to deny it and to try to get away from it. When our escapist tactics fail we are faced with the hard reality: what will we do with this event in our lives?

Cardinal Bernardin gave us an incredible model of how the Christian embraces the cross when he was unjustly accused of sexually abusing a young seminarian and later when he contracted cancer and eventually died. No words could ever describe how those false accusations broke the cardinal's heart! Nothing means more to a priest than his good name. Everyone knew that even after he was cleared, the doubts would always be there and would be used by his enemies.

The cardinal responded with such pure integrity and truthfulness that more and more people saw him as a transparent vessel of God's love. His forgiveness and reconciliation with Steven Cook are beautifully described in Cardinal Bernardin's *Gift of Peace.*

Cardinal Bernardin no sooner carried one cross when he was given another, which by his own admission was easier—terminal cancer. His embracing and carrying of this cross gave hope to countless people and their families who carry the cross of cancer. In the last phase of his life he became a brother to his sisters and brothers who had cancer. He visited cancer patients, celebrated healing Masses and reached out to all who were suffering. In the cross of cancer, Joseph Bernardin was the instrument of life and resurrection to many.

Sometimes instead of carrying our cross we drag it. We never really embrace it and it never becomes the instrument of life that it is meant to be for ourselves and for others. In this holy time when we walk with Jesus, He invites us to pick up our cross and walk with Him. It becomes so much lighter when we're willing to do that.

Third Station
Jesus Falls the First Time

We adore Thee O Christ and we bless Thee
because by Thy Holy Cross Thou hast redeemed the world.

MANY TRADITIONS speak of the falls of Jesus as he carried his cross. In this meditation let's look at this fall of Jesus and our falls as they symbolize discouragement and hopelessness.

In this fall Jesus experiences the terrible pain and embarrassment of an unprotected fall to the ground under the weight of the cross. This fall is endured by a man who has been savagely scourged, crowned with thorns and abused by cruel soldiers and onlookers. Think of how it feels to be treated like a nothing, to be laughed at, to be mocked and to have no one to defend your dignity.

The falls of Jesus remind and inspire us to work for and safeguard the dignity of each and every person. We must begin to see that when anyone is abused and treated as less than a human being, the pain and the embarrassment of Jesus continues.

The Church and the Christian are always called to be the defenders of the defenseless. We are expected to be there to speak out for the rights of those who have no one to speak on their behalf. The poor are always embarrassed. They wait and wait and wait for their turn. They are given the last and the worst of everything. No one makes a fuss about their children. No one tells them to take care of themselves or promises to send them a hot meal when they are ill.

The poor are Jesus lying flat on the ground, wounded and dirty, embarrassed and hopeless.

Perhaps this Lent we can work a little bit harder at treating everyone with politeness, dignity, concern, compassion and with our best manners. The simplest act of kindness to the least of His sisters and brothers is the most loving thing we can ever do for Jesus as He falls beneath the cross.

Lent is a wonderful time to practice more than charity to the embarrassed—to help create a world of justice where people will cease to be embarrassed because we have helped to lift the cross from their shoulders.

Fourth Station
Jesus Meets His Afflicted Mother

We adore Thee O Christ and we bless Thee
because by Thy Holy Cross Thou hast redeemed the world.

MARY MAKES HER WAY through the crowd to see her Son. When He finally walks past, her heart is broken. This is the first time she has seen Him since His arrest. The sight of her beautiful Son bleeding, lacerated and mocked breaks her heart. All that she can do is look at Him with all the love a

Mother can give. He looks at her and He is brokenhearted to know that His mother sees Him like this. Mary knows what it is to be powerless, to be unable to do anything to help her child.

This terrible scene is being lived out in the lives of so many parents who find themselves powerless to help their suffering children. Mary identifies with that vast number of holy women and men of all ages who would gladly lay down their own lives in place of their children.

How many parents see their children as slaves to drug abuse. They do everything, spend everything they have to save their children, but the hold of the drugs is too strong and they are forced to see their children destroy themselves by their lifestyle.

How many parents are like Mary as they look at and hold their children dying of AIDS, cancer and other diseases but are powerless to take away their pain and suffering.

Jesus continues to meet His mother in our world as so many parents look at their children in pain, injustice, prison, sickness, malnutrition, ignorance and neglect and can do nothing but try to be there for them and bear the pain with them.

Could there ever be more saintly people than parents whose hearts are broken because they are powerless to do something to aid their suffering children? These parents love their children as we love ours yet there is nothing they can do but suffer, love and die with them.

Dear mother Mary, we pray with you for all the holy saints, the parents who, like you, must watch their children walk to Calvary powerless to help them except with their look and touch of love.

Simon of Cyrene Helps Jesus to Carry His Cross

We adore Thee O Christ and we bless Thee
because by Thy Holy Cross Thou hast redeemed the world.

SIMON HELPS JESUS to carry His cross because Jesus is near total collapse under the weight of it. Simon is reluctant and would rather not get involved, but who can say no to the Roman soldiers.

Frequently, we are in Simon's shoes. We find ourselves doing good things, things that are truly virtuous, but sometimes our heart is not there. We are tired, discouraged and disillusioned. We are a lot like Simon—we don't really understand what we are doing or who we are helping.

Imagine how different Simon's attitude would have been if he had known who Jesus was! What was a burden and a great imposition would have become a privilege and a joy if only Simon knew that Jesus was the Son of God and that He was on His way to Calvary to perform the greatest act of love the world has ever known.

How different all of our burdens would become if we could truly understand the holiness of our lives, especially as we live out our commitments of love. So many parents are making heroic sacrifices to love and raise their children. So many adult children are patiently caring for their elderly parents in nursing homes, in hospitals or at home. So many spouses are at the bedside of their loved one day in and day out. They need to know that what they do each day as they minister God's mercy—lose sleep, nurse them,work endless hours—is the holiest thing they can ever do.

Their life is holy because like Simon they are carrying the cross for Jesus. They are touching, caressing and caring for Jesus as they serve their dear loved ones. Each person, after all, is Christ—to be loved, cherished and served. It is the great responsibility of the Church to remind her saints that they truly are saints and that all they do is holy. How rich and fulfilling all of our lives become when we realize that each of us actually carries the cross for Jesus as we live out our relationships with fidelity and love.

Each person we love, each person we meet, each opportunity of relating to another is another opportunity of great significance if, unlike Simon, we can believe that each person is a visitation of the Son of God and an invitation to love and serve Him.

Sixth Station
Veronica Wipes the Face of Jesus

We adore Thee O Christ and we bless Thee
because by Thy Holy Cross Thou hast redeemed the world.

THE STATION OF VERONICA wiping the face of Jesus and the face of Jesus imprinted on her veil is one that many of us recall with nostalgia and affection. It greatly impresses children as they visualize the tiny face of Jesus on Veronica's veil. The deep reality that it communicates only reaches us much later in life. This station teaches us the power and the beauty of the simplest act of love. In reality, it is what life and love are all about, and what gives meaning to our lives.

The life and death of Mother Teresa powerfully impressed the world with the beauty and the meaning of a single act of charity. That single act gives inspiration to the second, and so on, until we have grown accustomed to caring for and loving one another. Mother Teresa spoke of how important it was when she picked up the first dying man in the streets of Calcutta. She said that if she had not picked up that first person, she would not have picked up the second and all those who followed.

It can be frightening and discouraging to think of a life of service. How can I continue to love for ten or twenty years or more? How can I always be patient and forgiving to everyone? I don't have to be. I have to love one person at a time. As Mother Teresa said: "one, one, one, one..."

When I drive to work today there will be plenty of chances to be patient. I can be kind to some *one* at work. I can listen to the elderly person telling me the same story for the hundredth time. I can give some *one* the benefit of the doubt. I can *really* listen to my children. I can reach out to my spouse, even when I am tired. I can try to be patient with the couple preparing for marriage whose main concern is whether the church provides a runner for their wedding.

One, one, one, one—Jesus help me to believe that the face upon Veronica's veil is the face of each person I meet today. Help me to really care, to really extend my hand, to look into the eyes of the other person and see their pain and their struggle. Dear Veronica, pray for me that I will know that when I perform the simplest act of kindness, I do it to the Lord Jesus.

Seventh Station
Jesus Falls the Second Time

We adore Thee O Christ and we bless Thee
because by Thy Holy Cross Thou hast redeemed the world.

IN THIS STATION the humiliated, tortured and exhausted Jesus falls the second time. The second fall of Jesus will serve as a reflection on the reality of our own human frailty and weakness.

We all fall so many times. For some this becomes a terrible burden and embarrassment. They struggle with the sins and weaknesses of their youth all through their lives. They never reach the point in their lives when they have conquered the demons of their past. We battle with them; we win some battles but never conquer them all. All of this can seem very bleak to those who were taught that unless they were perfect God would not love them.

God loves us as we are. We do not earn His love. We can never deserve it. It is a gift. It is the gift of a loving Father who delights in His beloved children. We are the crowning glory of His creation and we are sinful. We will never have it all together and we will never stop struggling.

We never reach perfection and that's fine. We're not capable of reaching it. What pleases our God is that we never give up and we never stop struggling. Our holiness is in the struggle. We never give up but we always get up. We take His hand and begin again. That is what Lent is all about. That is what the Paschal Mystery means: we die to what binds us so that we may rise to new life, only to fall again and rise again and again.

A saint is a sinner who never gives up. Every saint has a past and every sinner has a future in Christ Jesus our Lord. St. Paul would say: "Therefore I glory in my weakness ...for when I am weak, then I am strong" *(2 Corinthians 12:10).*

I am indeed strong when I realize that Christ, not myself, is my strength. I am indeed strong when I hand my sins and weaknesses to Jesus and tell Him that He must help me because I can't do it alone. He will never abandon us. He understands the desires, pulls, obsessions, wounds, dreams, love and hate in each one of our hearts and He loves us just as we are. When we fall like Jesus did, He is there to help us up again.

Eighth Station
Jesus Comforts the Women of Jerusalem

We adore Thee O Christ and we bless Thee
because by Thy Holy Cross Thou hast redeemed the world.

JESUS IS COMFORTED by the loving ministry of these holy women who show Him compassion and mercy on His way to Calvary! He in turn comforts them by His gratitude and love. Notice Jesus did not stop to comfort and be comforted by the men of Jerusalem. The men of Jerusalem condemned Him to death and carried out the order.

How cold, heartless, merciless and cruel the world and the Church would be without the presence and the ministry of women. The women of the world seem to have a more natural ability to reflect the compassion and tenderness of God.

The women on the Via Dolorosa weep real tears for Jesus. They no doubt were disciples who heard Him preach many times and who believed in the kingdom He was trying to establish, a kingdom of peace, love and justice. They hoped for the new order that Jesus preached where their children would be cherished, loved and cared for. The kingdom of Jesus is the place where children, all children, would be safe.

These holy women truly loved Jesus and their hearts broke to see the Innocent One degraded in this terrible way. The holy women of today continue to weep over Jesus as He is scourged, abused and murdered in the person of their husbands, parents and children. The great sins of inhumanity seem to be committed by the men of our world and suffered by the women.

In our Church most acts of compassion are performed by women who are deeply committed to the Church and the world. In our parishes the vast majority of all work is done by women. They care for our poor, teach our children, visit the sick and homebound. They do the sacramental work of loving and nurturing the flock of Jesus. They do it with generosity and dedication in a Church reluctant to treat and accept them. Imagine where our Church would be —where our world would be—without our women!

The Church needs so much more of the feminine. Those in power need to learn how to weep with and for the broken of the world rather than trying to rule and control them. May the holy women of today pray that we may all acquire hearts of flesh and compassion so that we can all be there to comfort Jesus as He carries the cross to Calvary today.

Ninth Station
Jesus Falls the Third Time

We adore Thee O Christ and we bless Thee
because by Thy Holy Cross Thou hast redeemed the world.

IN THE THIRD and final fall of Jesus we sense despair in Him. He seems to be saying: "I can't go on any more. I've given everything I have. There's no more left." The feeling is similar to the moments in the garden where Jesus begs the Father to let the cup pass Him by. The garden scene and the third fall are the most terrible and loneliest moments that Jesus has to endure. They seem to be meant for us when we reach the end of our rope and just can't go on any more. We have a Savior who is Jesus and who has been there before us.

Very often the picture we receive of Christianity is that it is the religion of the rich, the intelligent, the powerful and the influential. We have romanticized Bethlehem to the point that we don't smell the animal manure or see the poverty of a homeless couple. We have done the same to the cross. Our Cecil B. DeMille scenery and costumes make the crucifixion a play in which Jesus *plays* a part, but after all, He *knows* He will rise, doesn't He? No, I don't think He does, anymore than you and I know we will get through the crucifixion in our own lives.

Jesus in the third fall identifies with those who have lost all hope and don't know where to turn. I have been privileged to share some of those moments with God's special saints. The parents who have lost a child know what Jesus' Passion is all about. He reaches out to them and to the women whose sons and husbands are waiting on death row. That convict waiting to be executed has a friend in Jesus who understands.

In His fall, Jesus embraces those wasting away with AIDS. He holds their families whose hearts are broken. As He falls, Jesus is the friend of the tortured souls suffering from mental illness. As he falls the third time and when He is sweating blood in the Garden, Jesus is as close to a nervous breakdown as one can get. He understands mental illness.

Yes, our Jesus, the Divine Physician has come and has endured all these things not for the healthy, the rich or the beautiful, but for us who reach moments in which we have lost all hope and do not know where to turn. These are moments when we would rather be dead. These are the moments when there is someone who is there reaching out to take our hand. It is Jesus.

Tenth Station
Jesus Is Stripped of His Garments

We adore Thee O Christ and we bless Thee
because by Thy Holy Cross Thou hast redeemed the world.

IN THIS TERRIBLE SCENE Jesus is stripped naked. His last bit of human dignity is ripped away as He is left to be looked upon by one and all. Every semblance of privacy is denied Him. The loin clothes that we see in most depictions of the crucifixion are really accretions dictated by the modesty of Christian artists. Our Jesus has everything taken from Him as he becomes the suffering servant of Isaiah 42—the Lamb of God led to the slaughter.

Our society revels in humiliating people and depriving them of their God-given dignity. Millions upon millions live in inhuman conditions in the slums of our great cities. So many grow up and live and die never knowing the most basic sanitation and hygiene. Christ continues to be humiliated as His sisters and brothers continue to live in such deplorable conditions all over the world.

As the pornography industry booms and earns billions of dollars of profit, it does so at the expense of victims, mostly women, who are exploited by this obscene business. No matter that they are a willing group who are selling the most intimate physical part of themselves. To do this even to willing victims is to exploit, debase and dehumanize these poor people beyond imagining. This stripping relegates a woman to being a thing, a commodity to be used and abused. Pornography strips people of every spiritual and intellectual quality, and sends a message to our youth that sex is no more than animal satisfaction. All thoughts of the relational and truly spiritual aspects of sex are robbed.

As sick as pornography is, the stripping of Jesus reaches its most diabolical proportion in the abuse and exploitation of children. Children are personally abused in the sex industries of the Orient that cater to well-healed Westerners coming for the "thrill" of having children to satisfy them. Here at home we give in as we allow the media to rob our children of their childhood by the garbage that is routinely transmitted on TV and in so much contemporary music.

All of this is not really about sex. It is about the responsibility we have as Christians to respect the dignity of each person and never to allow anyone, especially a child, to be used as a thing. This respect must begin with ourselves as we try to place our sexuality under the Lordship of Jesus. The power and force of lust become redeemed as we grow into people of tenderness, warmth and compassion. The Risen Christ calls us to that new life.

Eleventh Station
Jesus Is Nailed to the Cross

We adore Thee O Christ and we bless Thee
because by Thy Holy Cross Thou hast redeemed the world.

THE WOUNDS OF JESUS have been the source of meditation and prayer all through the years. Religious communities in the Church have been founded to meditate upon and preach the love of Jesus exemplified in His wounds.

As we meditate upon these holy wounds we can begin to understand their meaning and challenge to us today. To be a disciple of Jesus one must be as the Master was, one must bear the same wounds of love on our own person.

The wounds that we bear are the signs of love that we have given to one another. Our holy wounds symbolize the love, humility and service that we have given to others in the name of Jesus. The life of the Christian is marked by loving concern and care of others. In all of our vocations we are called upon to lay down our lives in service and in love.

The call to bear the wounds of Jesus began in a special way at the Lord's Supper as Jesus washed the feet of the Apostles. They found that experience so embarrassing because Jesus was defining for them what ministry, service and priesthood would mean in His Church. Jesus made it clear that His Church was never to be one of titles, privileges and honors contrary to the very meaning of the New Testament and especially the crucifixion. It's hard to understand sometimes what has happened to a Church where titles, prestige and power have become so important. As the Church needs to be reformed institutionally, so must we be personally reformed. Our following of Jesus must be a living out of His wounds by humility, service and compassion to others.

The greatest glory of God is the countless number of dedicated followers of Jesus who are living the woundedness of Jesus. So many parents, spouses, children, priests, sisters, deacons, friends and lay ministers live out in tender love and compassion the wounds of Jesus Christ. These holy ones save the Church and change it from a bureaucratic institution of little people looking for big honors to a loving and caring family looking for peace, justice, compassion and love for all people.

At the moment of our death Jesus will ask us to show Him our hands. If they are wounded by a life of service He will smile and say: "Welcome Home."

Twelfth Station
Jesus Dies on the Cross

We adore Thee O Christ and we bless Thee
because by Thy Holy Cross Thou hast redeemed the world.

THE TWO most moving religious depictions in the whole history of Christian art are the birth of Christ and His death. I suppose these two moments in His life are the ones we most identify with—we are all born and we shall all die—no exceptions. As we dwell upon the mystery of Jesus identifying with us in all things, His birth and His death become very significant to us. But what gives us most consolation in the death of Jesus is the love it symbolizes. It is at the foot of the cross that we learn the lessons of life and death.

So many times in my life as a priest people have said to me things like: "Does Jesus really love me, even with all my sins?" Down deep so many people believe that God's love must be earned. I have to be worthy of it. Coupled with this deep erroneous understanding of grace are the pain and wounds of human life—especially sin.

It is impossible for many people to believe that they can ever be forgiven for abortion, adultery, murder, child abuse, leaving the church, etc. For many, the project of atoning or making up for these sins is beyond their capability. How, then, could they ever be forgiven? How could they make up for a life of sin?

The only answer that I can ever give or that would ever make any sense to anyone is to simply ask the person to look at the cross and to ask Jesus to tell them what His death means. If we listen with our heart we will hear Jesus telling us that His love is greater than any of our sins. In His blood they are all washed away and we are His new creation.

Jesus on the cross forgives all of our sins. His love has no limit. We all have hope because He loves us without limit. The love of Christ will never be earned by anyone. No one is worthy of this love. We are all sinners. This love is a pure and simple gift. We can do nothing to be worthy of it. All we can do is accept it and celebrate it.

In our Lenten confession we will stand at the foot of the cross, look at the Son of God who loves us and forgives us without conditions and celebrate this love. In His love all our sins are washed away and though they be as red as scarlet they become white as snow.

Jesus Is Taken Down from the Cross and Is Laid in the Arms of His Mother Mary

*We adore Thee O Christ and we bless Thee
because by Thy Holy Cross Thou hast redeemed the world.*

Our Lady of Sorrows

I THINK the most moving of all religious images is that of Michelangelo's Pieta. The tender and poignant depiction of the Mother holding in her arms the dead body of her Son has the power to touch everyone's heart. This depiction of Mother and Son is more than a Lenten or even Christian symbol. It is universal in what it depicts and in what it says. While it powerfully depicts the pain, agony, sorrow and desperation of Mary holding her beloved Jesus, it also depicts Mary in her role of every woman, powerfully experiencing the agony and pain of modern woman.

The Pieta is so powerful because it does not depict Mary in glory, but in agony. It does not depict the beautiful and tender image of Mary and Child surrounded by angels and clouds. Rather it presents the other Mary—sitting alone on a dung heap holding her dead Son. No one is there to glorify them or worship them. No one cares if Jesus lives or dies. He's a nobody now. He's a zero. He has no followers, no magic, nothing. If Jesus is a nothing, what about His Mother!

The Pieta is the most moving of all the depictions of Mary. It is so powerful because in it she is totally powerless. Michelangelo is telling us through his art that Mary is one with the poor, the despised, the powerless and the unwanted.

Mary is sister and mother to all the women who wait and suffer with their sons and husbands as they await execution on death row. Just like Mary, they are the only ones there to hold and bury them after their execution.

Mary is the sister and mother of all those women who have suffered abuse and disrespect of all kinds. She is one with all women as they yearn for the respect and rights that they deserve and are so often denied. She is the woman raped and discarded in the former Yugoslavia. She is the child forced into prostitution in the Far East to satisfy the perverse appetites of rich westerners. Mary is the sister and mother of all women who are exiled. She left her country once because of the cruelty and injustice of Herod. Today millions of her daughters—children in arms—are forced to leave their countries and homes, perhaps never to return.

Mary is the sister and mother of the millions of political prisoners, the "disappeared" of Central and South America, the murdered and disposed innocent victims of ethnic cleansing and political expediency. She is the Rachel of today weeping for her children, but inconsolable because they are no more.

Mary is the sister and mother of all those women who have to face unplanned pregnancies. Mary chooses life–the life of this world—and she is there to support her troubled sisters and to tell them that they, too, carry within themselves the Christ Child. Imagine where we would be if Mary had chosen to destroy her child rather than bear Him! Yet, that is what happens when a woman terminates a pregnancy. She is one with her sisters as they make their decisions. She prays that they will choose life, but she loves them and prays for them when they choose another way.

Mary is the sister and mother of women whose children are rejected because of their color, nationality, religion or because they are poor. Mary reminds our society how we must share our gifts with the poor of the world—especially the children. She calls us to peace and a world where children will never suffer the ravages of war or poverty.

Mary is the sister and mother of all humanity. She is "every sister" and "every mother." She is the new Eve. Her role is to be advocate of all, especially the poor and the suffering. All the pain, fear, doubt, anger, loneliness and abandonment that a modern woman may experience, Mary has already experienced. All of the tears that are shed today by women have already been shed by Mary.

Mary is not the marble statue, clean and neat and tidy, emotionless and asexual, often seen depicted in our churches. Mary is the vulnerable, feeling, passionate woman who is the mother/sister to all modern women, rich or poor, who suffer the pain of life and injustice in our world. Those who suffer the most, have in Mary a friend who knows what they are going through and who never ceases praying for them.

It is said that when Michelangelo finished his work, it looked so real that he struck it with his hammer and shouted: "Speak!" This Mary has not stopped speaking to the world. She has not ceased telling us that the Mother of God is not above us or beyond us or even better than we are. What she is still saying to us is that the Mother of God is our mother and our sister and that just as she holds her beloved Jesus in her arms she also holds us and will never let go of us, especially when we are in agony or pain.

Mary is the mother of the political prisoner who was executed for trying to cause a revolution. Could there ever be a bigger "loser," "zero," or "nothing," than the mother of a dead criminal? No one wants to know her or be with her. No one wants to speak to her or look at her. She is despised. She doesn't matter. She's a throwaway. The Mother of God is a throwaway. She suffers everything so that all people— but especially women—will know that she not only understands their pain, but she has gone through it herself. She is not a statue in a safe niche. She is woman.

In the season of Lent we observe Mary as she comforts

Jesus in His Passion and death. The real tragedy is not that Jesus once suffered, but that He continues to bear the Passion in His suffering sisters and brothers. Mary is still with Him as she comforts and holds Him in the least of His sisters and brothers. Our call is to bring the Passion to an end by working for justice for all of our sisters and brothers.

Fourteenth Station
Jesus Is Placed in the Sepulcher

We adore Thee O Christ and we bless Thee
because by Thy Holy Cross Thou hast redeemed the world.

THE LOVING GESTURE of Joseph of Arimathea in giving his grave to Jesus says so much and gives us so much to pray about. Jesus dies a pauper. Not only are His clothes robbed; not only does He die as an executed criminal with just His mother and a few others present; he doesn't even own a grave. He is buried through the kindness of a distant admirer. Jesus dies as He lived—a poor man—with no possessions, no property and seemingly no accomplishments. *"Blessed are you who are poor for the Kingdom of God is yours..."* (Luke 6:20).

So many people die like Jesus—with nothing and with nobody—except with Jesus there to take them home to the Kingdom of Heaven. As we look at our lives and deaths to come, perhaps Jesus is reminding us with His borrowed grave that we are too concerned with material things and not enough concerned with people, love, relationships and our relationship with God.

We are all called to be poor. We are called to share our substance with those who have little or nothing. We are called to rate our success not in how much we own but in how much we love and are loved in turn. It is not a question of how much we have or don't have, but where our treasure and our heart truly are.

The call to be poor differs for each person. Parents will practice real poverty especially as they send their children to college and pay tuition bills! But parents who truly live the spirit of Jesus teach their children by example that the purpose of college is not to make as much money as you can, but to change the world through the gift of one's love and service to the human family.

For me, personally, the tension of the goodness of creation and things and the call to Gospel simplicity is very great. It is never really answered. I know I need things to do my work. I need a car. I need a vacation. These things are all good. Food and wine and clothes are wonderful—yet there is also the call of Jesus to be poor and the reminder that He didn't even own a grave. Such thoughts will never allow us to become puffed up or holier than Thou. We will always be in the process of becoming poor.

Everyday I am humbled by my people who live true evangelical poverty, making sacrifices beyond my comprehension as they give up everything in raising their children.

St. Francis was so in love with all creation but was called by God to give up every material thing. The Prayer of St. Francis will help us to figure out how much is enough. I pray that I may someday achieve a fraction of their dedication and commitment to the Lord.

Fifteenth Station
The Resurrection

We adore Thee O Christ and we bless Thee
because by Thy Holy Cross Thou hast redeemed the world.

IN THE RESURRECTION of Jesus all life and reality are changed forever. Sin and death are destroyed and the power of evil is once for all vanquished by the power of love. The war is won and God is the victor. It is true that there are many battles that still must be fought, but the victory is ours in Christ Jesus our Lord.

When the Church celebrates the Lord's resurrection she is celebrating the promise of Jesus that each of us shares in a new life that will never come to an end. This resurrection of Jesus is more than a treatise in a theology book. In the old theology manuals the resurrection of Jesus was the greatest "proof" of His divinity. The Resurrection is more than a proof. It is the core reality of Jesus and we are called to be the witnesses of this beautiful event in our own lives. The divine life is not just forever; that is the least important part of it. The divine life is a way of being, impossible without divine intervention in our own lives. It means sharing in and living the very life of the Blessed Trinity. The Easter sacraments of Baptism and Eucharist celebrate this new life and this abundant and glorious life which is ours forever. The only "proof" of the divinity of Jesus is the loving witness that we live to the resurrection of Jesus by our own personal resurrections from death to life.

We best witness the Resurrection of Jesus by truth, hope and service. Of course, it is love that permeates this witness.

The person who witnesses the Resurrection is the person of truth. The person of truth is transparent—the love and beauty of Jesus shines forth in them as every part of their life is filled with the presence of Jesus. There is never anything done in shadows or in darkness. The brightness of their light shines forth in all they do and in all they are. For this witness, there is never fear or any reason to hide anything. Their whole life is a witness that God lives and that love is stronger than hate. The lie is crushed by the power of truth, which is Jesus.

The person who witnesses the Resurrection is the person of hope. In all that they do, they know that God is present and that God leads and will take care of everything as long as we work with Him and live as His disciples. This hope is not the foolish and mindless hope of the Pollyanna. It is a sober and realistic hope that is very aware of the evil and sin that surrounds us, but knows that love is stronger than hate and that the God of Love will lead and care for His People. The witness of the Resurrection brings hope because he/she believes in the spirit of St. Paul expressed in Romans VIII: *"All things work together unto good for those who love God."*

Our world has never needed this hope more. No matter how challenging the problems of this world are (and they can seem overwhelming), good men and women working together are able to solve them. There is hope if we love one another and work together to build the Lord's Kingdom.

The witness of the Resurrection lives a life of humble service. Jesus is never more present than in the loving touch of the servants of Jesus. These servants were well taught and formed by the One who came to serve and not to be served. Jesus at the Last Supper celebrated the sacrament and then demonstrated what Eucharist should mean in the life of the Church, especially the clergy. Eucharist means washing the feet of our sisters and brothers.

The death of Mother Teresa was a beautiful celebration of her loving and humble service to humanity. It also confirmed and celebrated the loving service of countless disciples of Jesus—mothers and fathers, husbands and wives, sisters and brothers, nuns, deacons, priests and bishops, bartenders, cab drivers, garbage men, teachers, nurses, waiters, doctors, etc.—who witness the Resurrection through their loving and simple service. The list goes on and on as the saints all over this world give witness through their loving service that Jesus Christ is risen. They affirm a life that is so beautiful. It is the life of love, it is the kingdom of God. Alleluia!

7.

The Seven Last Words of Jesus

WHEN JESUS WAS CRUCIFIED He hung on the cross for three hours. The Scriptures record Jesus speaking at seven different times. The seven last "words" of Jesus have been the source of rich meditation and deep prayer over the centuries. At St. Brigid's Church it is customary for our people to preach the meditations on Good Friday at the beautiful service of the Seven Last Words. The depth of their relationship with Jesus becomes very apparent as they preach. Their lives of loving service give witness to the resurrection of Jesus and they inspire and challenge all of us who hear them to love Jesus more and to serve Him in all of our sisters and brothers.

Their preaching also assures us that like them our job isn't over yet. We are all in the process of becoming what Jesus wants of us. Our holiness is not in perfection. None of us will ever achieve that. Think of how boring we and life would be if we were all perfect! No, holiness consists in fidelity to Jesus. We fall often, but we get up and we never give up. It is in the getting up and taking of Jesus' hand that we find our Redeemer. That Redeemer never casts us aside, but rather loves us even more when we need Him and reach for His hand.

The most intimate and loving moment in the lives of St. Peter and the Apostles was when Jesus forgave them for their denial, cowardice and abandonment during His Passion and Crucifixion. I hope the holy women didn't gloat too much about their own courage, affirmation and fidelity to Jesus during those terrible moments. They certainly had a right to—after all, the men were nowhere to be found.

It is with great pride and joy that I now introduce to you some very special friends as they guide us through the Seven Last Words of Jesus on the cross. I cannot begin to tell you what a privilege it is to work side by side with such holy people who love me, inspire me, encourage me and challenge me to be a Christian and a priest. I am in awe of their holiness, their sacrificial lives of service and their love. The greatest treasure the Church has is its own people. Let us pray that the Church will come to appreciate them and allow them to exercise their priesthood in building up the Body of Christ.

First Word
"Forgive them Father!
They Don't Know What They Are Doing"

by Linda K. Schoenberg

WHAT DO I KNOW of forgiveness? Forgiveness is probably one of the most difficult things for me to deal with; I have a hard time with the very concept and definition of it!

Oh sure, I can forgive friends and co-workers who have hurt my feelings unintentionally. I can forgive many, many things that people do or say unthinkingly or unwittingly— things which hurt me directly or indirectly or which make my life a little more difficult.

But the key word here is "little." Those things that make my life a little more difficult are forgivable. But some things, I feel aren't mine to forgive. Some things are too big, too painful, and too shameful, and I think forgiving them is too tall an order for me to handle. These are things that

God's got to forgive—plain and simple.

Well, that's my off-the-cuff view of forgiveness. I guess Fr. Frank asked me to meditate and pray with Jesus for a good reason! I've sat with Jesus dying on the cross. What a horrible, shameful, humiliating thing, dying on a cross between two thieves. And yet, through it all, Jesus asked the Father for forgiveness for the people who condemned Him and carried out His sentence. "Forgive them, Father. They don't know what they are doing."

I've asked Jesus how He can forgive these people, and really, what does He mean by forgiveness anyway?

Really, what *does* forgiveness mean? Does it mean that "everything is OK?" You know, forgive and forget! Does that mean that if a rapist say's he's sorry, the rape doesn't count? If a child-molester says, "I'm sorry," the kid should forget it, and act as if it didn't happen? If a friend or relative betrays or abandons you, you should just shrug your shoulders and say, "It's OK, you're forgiven. No problem!" and just move on? I don't know, this forgiveness thing is a tough one.

Jesus was nailed to a cross. He was beaten and mocked, denied by His friends, and yet He forgave them. But wait a second. Did *Jesus* forgive them? Did He say, "I forgive you! You don't know what you are doing?" No! Jesus, the only begotten Son of the Father, the Son of Man, rabbi, son, friend, was betrayed by one of his closest cohorts. Lord Jesus, whose divinity and humanity I believe in with all my heart and mind and soul, did not say, "I forgive you!" He implored His Father, our Father, to do the forgiving.

Lord Jesus, the Second Person of the Holy Trinity, was very, very human! And Jesus, the human being, in the last moments of His life on earth as a human being did not, probably could not, forgive these people by Himself! Jesus, who taught us to love one another as He has loved us, could not, it seems to me, forgive these people on His own. No matter how much love Jesus had for these people, He did not travel the road to forgiveness by Himself; He traveled the road with the Father!

My lesson in this is that I, too, am a human being. Just like Jesus, the human being, I have limits. There are things that I cannot do myself. But like Jesus, I can ask for help. How lucky I am to have a God who is there to help me! My struggles are burdens that I don't have to shoulder alone.

And part of my struggle is to recognize and accept my humanness. It sometimes seems so much easier to think that I can do everything by myself. But the reality is that I'm not really that powerful. And truthfully, if I give myself a break, I may give myself a chance to see that it really isn't easier to haul the whole burden alone. Sharing the load with a willing partner really is easier than doing it by myself. But I have to be willing to do it! And God is always so willing to help!

God, I've been told, forgives all of our sins. But what does that mean? If I pray to him to forgive me, am I asking Him to do something? Am I asking Him to make me feel better? If I forgive somebody for something or ask God to forgive that person, what am I really asking for?

When I go to confession, I say what I've done and I say that I'm sorry. My goal is to make amends for what I've done. So I can understand forgiveness, in that context. But what about forgiving people for things that they are not sorry for, are not aware of having done? "They don't know what they are doing." So how do I forgive them or ask for them to be forgiven?

I came to St. Brigid's when I had reached bottom— emotionally, physically, and spiritually, I had hit absolute zero. Doctors couldn't help me, anti-depressants could not treat the symptoms of my illness; they could do nothing to cure the disease.

My disease manifested itself as I began to deal with some very big, very painful, and very shameful truths about my past. I had visited with a relative whom I hadn't seen in a very long while, and shortly after our visit, I was racked by memories of abuses which occurred while I was in elementary school. I can't describe the feelings and physical symptoms that I experienced, but believe me when I say that I really felt that I had nowhere to turn, nowhere to go. Counseling was helping, but I needed something more. As a last resort, I asked a friend to take me to church. The rest is history. At St. Brigid's I was reborn spiritually and welcomed into the Church family last Easter.

I mention these "trespasses against me," to illustrate why my head still insists that there are some things that I just can't forgive yet. I say "yet" because I have not learned everything there is to learn from Jesus. And this forgiveness thing is still a struggle for me. A little less of a struggle than before, but still not an easy task.

Jesus tells us to love one another as He loved us. The love that He had for His friends is probably what compelled Him to seek forgiveness for these people. Jesus left us peace; He gave us His peace. Perhaps the goal of forgiveness is peace of mind – freedom from the hold others' evil deeds have on us. Perhaps, someday, with God's help, I too, will be able to say, "Forgive them, Father."

"Today you will be with me in Paradise. This is my solemn promise."

by Maureen and Rick Tufano

Rick

JESUS, YOU PROMISED me from your cross that **"Today, I shall be with you in Paradise."** I feel unworthy of your solemn promise. I feel humbled by the love which you continue to bestow on me, even in your pain, your suffering and your loneliness. How is it that you are still able to forgive me in the midst of all your suffering? Jesus forgive me for the times when I have not loved the way you have commanded me to love. I especially ask your forgiveness for the many times I have hurt you deeply by hurting my Maureen, the lover whom you have given me to be the sign of your love for me on earth. The woman who has promised to love me into heaven.

Jesus I feel ashamed because I have been such a poor steward of the love you have entrusted to me through your sacrament of matrimony. Too many times I have failed to cherish my Maureen. My shame is like being caught betraying a trust out of laziness—like a trusted guard found asleep on his watch. I pray that your presence in our sacrament will be as real to me as your presence to the repentant thief. Bless us with the grace to forgive each other the way you have forgiven this thief, with compassion and total acceptance. Jesus, help me to be the perfect lover, help me not to hurt the person you have put on this earth who has vowed to love only me until death do us part. Give me patience to continue to love her and forgive her even though I may fail time and time again to love as you have commanded me.

Maureen

DEAR JESUS, today you died so that I could one day be with you in Paradise. I feel so overwhelmed and unworthy of your sacrifice, yet blessed and cherished because of your infinite love. And even as you lay dying on the cross, your love and forgiveness was unwavering and all-encompassing. Even when I'm not all you call me to be, when I forget that you are the center of my life, when I act as though I am capable of doing anything without you, you don't give up on me. You always have your arms open, calling me back to you, to your love, to your promise of paradise. I'm never the perfect child, but you are the perfect parent, accepting all of me and showing me how to love through your example. Yet, how often have I let you down, dear Jesus, in not loving the way I should? My heart is so heavy talking to you about this Lord and I feel full of shame for not fully valuing the gift of your pure love in the person of my Rick. When you blessed our marriage, you gave our love relationship meaning and purpose and gave me Rick to love and cherish from that day forward. Yet, too many times, I've failed to love him with the kind of love I promised him, and You, on our wedding day. I know your words of the promise of Paradise call me to make changes in my life and in my relationship with Rick, with trust and belief in the power of your love for us. Please fill me with the strength of your grace so that I can be all you call me to be, for Rick and for you.

Rick

MAUREEN, ON OUR WEDDING DAY I promised before Jesus to love you until my dying day. Today, I acknowledge to you and to Jesus the many times I have not fully lived up to that vow. I am asking you not only to love me but to forgive me for all the times I've hurt you, for all the cruel words I've said to you, and for all the kind words I've failed to say to you. Forgive me for taking you for granted and for failing to listen to you with my heart when you were brave enough to love me and speak to me from your heart. Forgive me for looking at you but not seeing the deep love and devotion that you have for me. Maureen, I don't deserve your forgiveness for these things that I have done, but I stand before you and before Jesus today and ask your forgiveness.

Maureen

RICK, WITH JESUS' DYING WORDS of forgiveness as my example, I forgive you from my heart, for any time you've hurt me. Your words or actions may have made me feel unimportant to you or misunderstood at times but I love you more than life itself and I thank Jesus every day for His most wondrous gift of you in my life. Your love is constant, faithful and true, and I take that love with me always and everywhere. I vow to forgive you and love you the way Jesus asks me to, to love you so that you grow and become more and in loving you this way, I can love you into heaven.

Rick

MAUREEN, YOUR FORGIVENESS makes me new and humbles me. Thank you for your great love and for this forgiveness which I don't deserve but cherish so much. Your forgiveness makes Christ real to me in our sacrament. When I look at you I see Christ and my heart rejoices in the gifts he has bestowed upon me, especially your deep and unwavering love. Thank you Jesus for this gift you have given me in Maureen. Help me to live my sacrament and be the witness of your love and forgiveness through your presence in our relationship. Jesus, I vow to you that I will love my beloved Maureen into heaven.

Maureen

RICK, YOUR FAITHFULNESS, patience and forgiveness are signs of your love, of Christ's love. Your love is a blessing I couldn't live without, and today, I also ask you to love me enough to forgive me for all the hurts I've caused, for every time I've placed conditions on my love for you. Forgive me for failing to love you with the completeness of Jesus' love. I don't deserve your forgiveness but I place myself on my knees, asking, like the repentant thief on the cross, that you bless me with your love, with Jesus' love through your forgiveness.

Rick

MAUREEN, I FORGIVE YOU from my heart for any hurt you may have caused me. Even when your words were cruel and you may have rejected my love. I promise you that I will always keep on loving you. I will not be deterred from my love even if you doubt my love or if you reject me. I stand ready to always forgive you and to hold you in my arms and love you with Christ's tender love.

Maureen

THANK YOU JESUS, for the love you have given me in my beloved Rick. Thank you for your life, for your forgiveness, for your love and above all for your death so that we can live again with you in paradise.

Third Word
"Woman, behold your Son."

by Estelle C. Peck

"WOMAN, behold your son. Son, behold your mother."
Theologically, the third in the sequence of Jesus' final words from the cross are an expression of Jesus' concern for his

Church, as well as for his mother. Jesus knew that if Mary were to be alone without child or spouse, she would be considered cursed by her Jewish community. Therefore, in his deep love for her, Jesus entrusted Mary to his disciple, John, and in his deep love for his Church, John to Mary. Mary would not only be taken care of; all believers would be taken care of. Through this final deed of crucifixion, Mary becomes the Mother of all believers; Mary becomes our Mother. She does not take the place of Jesus; in no way does this humble, beautiful creature take the place of the Son of God. Through this simple, direct, loving gesture we are mothered for eternity.

As I prayed over these words of Jesus to his beloved Mother, I struggled with the imagery and the consequent feelings I feared would stir within me. For many years I followed Jesus to his death through child-like eyes and felt disturbed, even terrified, by the graphic images that haunted me. I didn't think too much about Mary and how she felt, though I felt sorry for her. I didn't know very much about motherhood when I was young.

As I matured, and as my faith matured with each passing Good Friday, I grew in my understanding of the Passion and death of Jesus. As I overcame my youthful sensitivity to the physical aspects of Jesus' Passion, I was gradually drawn into a growing love affair with Jesus and his Church, the Church given to Mary before he died. Not only my heart, but also my mind became engaged. I began to embrace and challenge the mystery of this cross in my own everyday life and in the broader world.

I also began to understand more fully the mother/child relationship between Mary and Jesus. The dialectic nature of this relationship was no different for Mary and Jesus than it is for all of us. Mother becomes child and child becomes mother. This loving contest between mother and child never really ends until the final moment of resurrection. It didn't end for Mary. It hasn't yet ended for me. And I'm sure it hasn't ended for you if your mother is still present in your life. But even though this great love story of Mother and Son became clearer to me with each passing year, it did take a long time for me to understand my own situation.

As a child and an adolescent, I was blind to my own goodness and self worth. Caught up in a world which afforded me all the material comforts I needed, I was afraid to ask for anything more. Yet there was always a void within me—a yearning for something more . . . a pervasive sadness. This feeling of never being good enough often propelled me into situations, which almost buried me. But there was something else which burned inside me—a toughness, a gnawing desire not to let go or to give up. Call it grace, call it faith, call it stubbornness—whatever it was, I believe it was God-given and I am grateful for it. Even though I was afraid of the God I knew then, I felt close to Him, and I believed He was real. As I grew into adulthood, God became even more real to me through a loving husband, wonderful children and beloved friends who cared for and about me and believed in me. The God I feared became my friend.

My adult imagination cannot even begin to comprehend Mary's anguish as she stood beneath her precious Son, Jesus, being crucified . . . wracked in pain, bleeding, moaning, screaming. Something so deep, so real, stirs within Mary to want to take Jesus' pain upon herself. "Put me up there instead of you. Take my blood. Put the nails through my hands and feet. Whip me, strip and humiliate me. Jesus, please let go. Go to your Father. God, how much longer must he endure this torture? Take my son into your arms," Mary pleads. "Let go, Jesus, please let go. You have done your work." Not yet, Mary, Jesus has not finished yet. Mary then remembers the prophet Simeon's words spoken some thirty-three years before when Jesus was a tiny babe in her arms: "A sword shall pierce your own soul." (Luke 2:35).

Meanwhile, John, Jesus' beloved disciple, is holding Mary, embracing her. Feeling helpless, he is doing his best to ease her agony. It's almost an hour now that Jesus has been up there on that splintered cross, but it seems like an eternity. There's a gasp of breath. Jesus is trying to speak. He looks deeply into the eyes of his beloved mother. How he adores her. His heart breaks for her as he speaks his words of love for her and the world: "Woman, behold your son. Son, behold your mother." How much he loves his mother . . . how much he loves us!

Though Mary knew Jesus' intentions better than anyone else, she did not always grasp the why of his actions. So Mary succumbs to the arms of John and remains with her beloved Son as he completes the greatest love story ever told. Simeon's prophecy to Mary is a prophecy to all mothers. There have been moments in my own motherhood when I did not understand the actions of my children. A piercing sword? Yes, a piercing sword. The evils of the world tried to get my children and me. But, love shielded their conquest. Thank you, Jesus. Thank you, Mary for teaching me what love really is—for widening my heart and clearing my mind to understand the power of love. I am so sorry you had to go through so much for me to learn.

Why does it take so long for us to understand? Why don't we get it? Hatred doesn't solve anything. Brutality, revenge, getting even, abusive power—it just continues the vicious cycle of misery. Why don't we teach our children when someone hits them not to hit back? There are other ways to solve disagreements. Retaliation just continues the vicious cycle. One country bombs, another bombs back. Someone has to stop it. Where does it get us? Destruction, poverty, disease, homelessness—misery—nothing but misery. Each and every minute of the day mothers are tortured by the anguish of watching their children starve to death because of the lack of proper nourishment. God provides the milk of the mother's breast, but greed and power halt the lifeline from God to mother to child. Yes, the Lord in his love has provided all that we need. But victims become victims because of the merry-go-round of selfishness and negativity. How can it end? Jesus and Mary make it so clear—love is the only answer—nothing else is needed. Love can fix anything and everything.

It has taken me a long time to understand the meaning of love, and I know I still have a lot to learn about it. My childish thoughts and feelings of the past still singe my heart and I know they will always be a part of me. But, that's okay. There is no one to blame. Now it's up to Jesus and me. And, as each Good Friday comes, as I confront another Passion, whether it be in Lent or any other day of the year, I know that Easter is soon to follow. Yes, Lord, I love you. And I love you too, Mary. Thank you for loving me so much.

Fourth Word
"My God, my God, why have you abandoned me?"

by Linda and Ken Roberts

NOTHING IN THE NEW TESTAMENT so clearly demonstrates to us the humanity of Jesus, as His last words, recorded in the Gospel of Matthew, *"My God, My God, why have you abandoned me?"* These words thunder with His pain.

He *was* on a cross.

He *had* been wounded.

He *had* been defiled.

He *had* been abandoned—save for those few women who never left Him.

And with His mortal life slipping away and pain

overwhelming Him—His mental faculties becoming clouded as the life force within Him diminished—we hear Him cry out: WHY!

His faith in God remains, but His human need to make sense of what has happened to Him screams for an answer.

As we reflected on His cry, *"My God, My God why have you abandoned me?"* the enormous impact of the word *abandon* struck us. Abandonment connotes helplessness and loneliness. Abandonment suggests victim—the abandoned child, the abandoned family, the fear all of us harbor of being left alone. This feeling of abandonment touches a fear in us because all of us have felt the pain of being abandoned.

Perhaps we gave been abandoned by a good friend.

Perhaps one of our parents has left us.

Some of us have been abandoned and left alone by a spouse.

Some of us have been abandoned by an employer.

Most of us have been abandoned by the death of someone we love, perhaps from illness, from an accident, or tragically from suicide.

Sometimes, we lose friends and family because God has called us to do something different—to follow a different path. In 1981, I began my journey of faith in Catholicism here at St. Brigid's. I had been called to follow a different path from my parents and my grandparents. My grandmother had come to this country in the early part of this century and went on to establish the Women's Lubbavatcher movement in Brooklyn—an ultra Orthodox Jewish sect. She had followed her path on her journey of faith, and I, fifty years later, had followed mine. But our faith journeys divided us. She felt that I had abandoned her and her faith. I felt that my grandmother had abandoned me.

Some have experienced the feeling of total abandonment when someone close to them attempts or actually commits suicide. I understand. As a young child, a child of ten, I watched my mother leave the house one day and not come back. I was confused. I was very scared. I felt alone. I felt totally abandoned and I felt very angry. I needed my mother, I wanted my mother, but she was gone. She was not there. As a little girl I asked the question "why" but there was no answer. My pain was real—my pain remains.

And as we think of Jesus, abandoned and alone on the cross and of so many others who are abandoned and alone—all trying to survive their terrible loneliness—how fortunate we are!

For 2,000 years—for 2,000 Lents—the answer to this difficult question has been before us.

Every year, it is again demonstrated. The answer, of course, is Easter!

"My God, my God, why have you abandoned me?" That question was answered on the *first* Easter, and every Easter since.

And for all of us, as we struggle with life—there is always refuge in Easter—always life reborn—always victory over death!

And each of us, in our eternal struggle to understand life, turns to the cross. We look at the cross and we think of Jesus. Jesus *was* a man. Jesus *was* human. And we all ask: "Why?" Why did He have to suffer and die on the cross?

The way to handle all of these "whys" is to continually fix our eyes on Christ's love displayed each Easter. And it is an essential truth of our faith that the triumph of Easter can never be far from our consciousness. It is important for us to remember that the answer to the "why" of Jesus' death is that His death provided us with the tools to conquer death. His death assures us that by prayer—the struggle to find God in the world—we can find the answers.

Fifth Word
"I am thirsty."

by Frank and Maureen Pesce

As FRANK AND I PONDERED and prayed over this scripture passage we tried to listen to the words of Jesus echoed in our lives. Our thoughts turned first to our three children, Jeannine, Danny and Joseph. Many times over the years we have heard the stillness of the night being disturbed by a small voice which says plaintively: "I am thirsty, Mommy." Or, "Daddy, may I please have a glass of water?" Through the bleariness of sound sleep we lovingly take care of our child's needs. But, of course we all know that the child is looking for more than just a glass of water. At moments like that a child is looking to make sure that Mommy and Daddy are still there. Although it is a glass of water that the child asks for, we know that our child thirsts for our love.

Maureen

As A NURSE I often hear these words of Jesus, "I am thirsty," echoed by my patients. Sometimes these patients are suffering terribly. Some are dying. As with Jesus, they seek a small measure of relief in the quenching of their thirst. Even those who have been given their medication and been assured by their doctor that they will be all right still seek comfort and relief from the ordeal of a hospital stay by asking for something to drink. Although they are asking to have their medical needs taken care of, I know they thirst for compassion.

Frank

As A LAWYER I spend much of my time listening to clients

telling me how they've been wronged. If I were to ask each one what he or she thirsted for I am sure they would say "justice." However, as many times as I listen, I realize that what they want is a chance to tell their story. What they want is for someone to listen to them. Although they come to me to have a legal problem solved, they are simply thirsting to be heard.

In these economically rough times we often hear the words "I am thirsty" uttered by those who are poor, hungry and homeless. They ask for food and drink to ward off the pangs of hunger and for decent paying jobs so they can afford the basic necessities of life. They seek shelter from the cruel cold, the relentless rain and the oppressive heat. But when they ask for these things—that so many of us take for granted—aren't they really asking for a chance to make it on their own? Aren't they really asking not to be forgotten and cast aside? They may ask for food, clothing, shelter and work, but in the final analysis they thirst for dignity and respect.

If we walk down just about any city street, or even if we turn on the news at night we cannot help but see one group or another protesting against some form of oppression. We cry out for equality.
- Perhaps we are the wrong color.
- Perhaps we speak the wrong language.
- Maybe we are the wrong gender.
- Maybe we are gay.
- Perhaps we are physically different. Maybe we cannot see or hear, or speak or walk.
- Perhaps we are simply too short or heavy.
- Maybe we are old.
- Maybe we practice our faith.

No matter what the situation, we want an end to discrimination. And sometimes we speak arrogantly, shout militantly. But we are really whispering, "I am thirsty...

thirsty for acceptance."

Today as we look at Jesus suffering on the cross and we hear him say, "I am thirsty," we might ask ourselves: "Is Jesus simply looking for something to moisten his parched lips, or is He, too, asking for something more?"

- Is Jesus, like the child in the night, asking for love?
- Is Jesus thirsting for compassion?
- Is he thirsting for dignity and respect?
- Is He thirsting for acceptance?
- Is Jesus thirsting for God?

If our answer is yes, then we must ask: Am I prepared to give Him all that He thirsts for?

- Am I prepared to give selfless love to my children, compassion to the sick and dying?
- Am I prepared to lend an ear to those who need to be heard?
- Am I prepared to offer dignity and respect to the poor, the hungry, the homeless?
- Am I prepared to accept those who are different?
- Am I prepared, deep in my heart, to give to each of my brothers and sisters – God's love?

Maybe—just maybe—this is why God waits three days to raise Jesus from the dead—to give me time to ponder these questions. To give me a chance to search my heart and say "Yes!" for it is only by saying a sincere and a heartfelt "Yes" to all of these questions that I am able to join in God's work of raising Jesus—His Son and our Brother—from the dead.

Sixth Word
"It is finished"

by Nick Tortorella

HOW IRONIC are these words of Jesus on the cross: "It is finished," or "It is accomplished." By our standards, what had

Jesus accomplished, what had He finished?

His closest friends, in His hour of greatest need, abandoned Him, or as kids say today, *dissed* Him.

He died poor and virtually alone, except for His mother and a couple of friends, who after His death went into hiding. Poor, abandoned, alone—not too successful I'd say!

Politically, He had no influence, in fact as He was being executed the soldiers and bystanders were laughing. I cannot imagine even the most callous among us laughing at an execution.

Our Lord is laughed at. As though what He had accomplished was laughable, silly. What a condemnation, what a failure. How unsuccessful He was!

Yet, Jesus' word is a word of victory, completion, accomplishment.

It's funny, in my own life accomplishment has always been an important thing. Being accomplished in school as a child, being accomplished in ministry, being an accomplished spouse, an accomplished father, an accomplished employee.

Yet, what is accomplishment really all about. At the moment of my own death, will I be able to echo the words of our Lord, "It is finished," "It is accomplished," with the same gentle peace that He did. Or will I continue to press for more, wanting more, never content with the now.

Lord, help me to focus on the right things. Help me to savor the many blessings you have given me, not simply search for more, fully knowing more is never enough. Help me to discover what it means to say with you, "It is finished, it is accomplished."

I don't believe that the Lord's words from the cross were just about His own mission. I believe that He was speaking about those He left behind. In spite of their humanity, their weaknesses, even their lack of faith, He saw in them a certain sense of accomplishment and hope.

I don't always appreciate the gifts and accomplishments of others. The Lord has blessed me with a wonderful wife. Yet, there are many times when I'm not content with the accomplishments of her day. It seems there is always more to do. One more chore, one more errand, one more task. I often focus on those things not finished, not accomplished. Yet, in my quiet moments on the train or in the car, I know I have a wife who has accomplished a great deal. Warm, loving, wise and a wonderful mother – she indeed is accomplished.

The Lord has blessed me with four wonderful children and I guess like many of us, I don't focus enough on their accomplishments, but rather on their shortcomings. You could have done better on that exam, your room could be cleaner, you could help more around the house. Yet, again in those quiet moments, I realize the Lord has blessed me with happy, healthy, loving and respectful kids. And if that is the most they ever achieve in life, how truly accomplished and blessed they are—and—am I.

The world I travel in, the world I live in, has a very different sense of the finish line, of accomplishment, then our Lord had. If I work harder, if I get ahead, I'll earn more, then I can do more and buy more and then accomplish more.

Lord, I'm on the carousel of life...slow me down.

I once heard a talk by Mother Teresa, that simple, beautiful woman of India. She offered simple, but poignant words to her audience that day—words that have stuck with me for many years, yet whose power has never penetrated my heart and mind completely.

She said, "God does not expect that we will be successful, God only expects that we will be faithful."

That's it! That's it, Lord! That's what you meant on the cross. "It is finished, it is accomplished, I have been faithful."

Lord, I spend a good deal of my time struggling to achieve, to accomplish, to finish successfully. But that's not what you're truly asking of me.

My prayer this day, this good day, this Good Friday is very simple: Lord, at the end of my days may I gently whisper your words, "It is finished, it is accomplished." And when I utter those words Lord, let them be about the right things, the simple things that truly equate to being faithful not successful. Help me Lord to be an accomplished spouse – loving, gentle, helpful, comforting, thoughtful. Help me Lord to be an accomplished father, brother, co-worker, friend, minister, disciple. That's all you expect, that's all you ask, that's all I need to accomplish. And Lord, if I can begin to really believe that, how much easier every day will be. May Jesus Christ be praised now and forever. Amen.

Seventh Word

Father, into Your hands I commend my spirit."

by Kevin Murtha

SUNDAY, FEBRUARY 2, was the Feast of the Presentation of Christ; the day St. Joseph presented the Infant Jesus to God the Father, giving thanks for his birth. My fourteen year old son John, an altar server, was preparing for his favorite activity—serving Mass. John had been shopping the previous day and picked out a special outfit.

It was a morning like many others with confusion and havoc as our family of six prepared for church. John stepped out of the shower. He combed his hair and put on his favorite cologne. He said he wanted to lie down because he was tired. "How do you feel, Buddy?" I asked. He whispered, "I'm fine." As the words passed his lips, the sparkle left his eyes and my son John died.

John had Down's syndrome and a defect in his heart.

Two weeks earlier his doctor told my wife and me that John's heart had reached the stage where he could die at any time —tomorrow or in ten years. John was in the room when the doctor gave us this news. He kept telling his mother to stop crying. John accepted his condition, and besides, the discussion was interrupting the television show he was watching.

After speaking to the doctor, I prayed that when that moment came, our family would be with John. I knew that no matter how traumatic his last moments were, John would gain great comfort in the fact that we were there. John would somehow feel that everything would be "fine."

My prayers were answered sooner that I had hoped and John, without any fear or fuss, commended his spirit into the hands of God. As with Jesus, John knew that his family was around him and that God in heaven awaited him.

As Jesus hung on the cross, mocked and humiliated, He was at peace with the knowledge that His death was part of God's plan. Jesus was human. He experienced terror and fear. Jesus experienced despair as He asked why His father abandoned Him. Yet, His feelings evolved into acceptance. Jesus gathered peace through acceptance and willfully gave His spirit to His Father. But how could Jesus have believed that part of God's plan was the death of His only son?

If I were born two thousand years ago, and I witnessed a man who was dedicated to helping and healing others—a man who set forth as the Son of God—being tortured, humiliated and degraded, I would have to feel "where is God now?" "What possible reason could there be for this horrible event?"

Could Jesus have realized how perfect God's plan was? Could Jesus have imagined that as a result of His death, there would be a Church, with communities, families, hospitals, schools and programs that give comfort and direction in the support and celebration of life?

Just as Jesus was at peace with God's plan and willingly gave His spirit to the Father, Jesus is telling me to accept the events in my life. He is asking me to commend my spirit into His hands and to encourage those around me to do the same.

Commending my spirit into God's hands doesn't mean accepting every event without question or intervention. It is not an excuse or escape. It means I must help others and myself to the best of my ability. If I see the dignity and rights of those around me being compromised, I must still fight to protect them. However, I must accept the results as part of God's plan. Jesus is asking me to be at peace with God.

When John was born I couldn't accept his condition. I could not willfully commend my spirit into God's hands. My wife and I were told that John probably wouldn't survive more than two years. Like Jesus, I felt abandoned. I felt as though I was on a cross. Over time, I commended my spirit into God's hands and I was at peace with John's condition. From that time forward, what was once a tragic event turned into the most beautiful experience of my life. John taught me acceptance, unconditional love, forgiveness and joy.

When John died I know he gave his spirit willingly to God but I felt as though God had abandoned me. Jesus is again telling me to accept God's plan and to give my spirit willfully, not just in death but in life. When we experience tragedy, depression, or when we have lost our direction, we must give our spirit to God, just as Jesus did.

When I accept my pain and help those who suffer, I serve God. If I can commend my spirit into God's hands, my heart will be at peace and my soul will achieve all the greatness and joy I could ever hope for.

8.

Experiences of Resurrection

IN EACH OF OUR LIVES Jesus allows us many experiences of His new life and resurrection. The love of another person, reconciliation with a family member, performing an act of charity, experiences like these remind us that Jesus is alive and that we share in His life.

Perhaps the most powerful experience of resurrection is the birth of a new child and the celebration of the sacrament of Baptism. But there are many couples who hear the Good Friday sadness of infertility. Our parish gathers these couples together twice a year to embrace them and to beg the Lord for the gift of resurrection—a child.

The experience of coming together is in itself an experience of resurrection because each couple knows that they are not alone—a pain shared with others is lessened and each is called to set aside their personal pain and reach out to another.

The very act of the Church embracing her beautiful children in pain is a touching and powerful sign of love and resurrection and can be the means for some to be reconciled with the Church.

At a recent Mass for these couples I invited two couples who were present at a previous Mass to give a testimony of their journey in faith. I know you will find both of these testimonies true and powerful experiences of resurrection.

Why Us?

by Colleen and Steve Rehm

GOOD EVENING, we would like to begin by thanking Father Frank for inviting us here tonight to honor St. Gerard and to share our story with all of you. My name is Colleen and this is my husband Steve. Last year Steve and I attended this Mass as an infertile couple. This year we attend as parents.

On July 1, our prayers were answered and our dreams came true when our son Steven was born. We do not come here this evening to brag, but to give hope. The path of infertility is long and hard and each month brings about incredible emotions and feelings. Throughout our struggle we found ourselves angry, distressed and wanting an answer to an impossible question: "Why us?" As time passed, our attitude toward each other and God changed. We found our relationship growing stronger as we leaned on one another through each monthly disappointment. Our feelings toward God went through many changes as well. At first we prayed for a child, then we demanded a child as if our desire for a child was being challenged and at times we even felt betrayed by God. We felt alone, as if God had turned His back on us. As time progressed we began to pray simply for strength – the strength to continue on our path, the strength to face disappointments and the strength to work together. It became clear that God had been providing us with His strength and hope all along by giving us His ear, His shoulder, and His wisdom in the form of a friend, family member and a doctor. As we now look at our son Steven it's quite clear: "Why us?"

We believe that God sent us on a difficult journey that He knew we could handle. I offer this belief to all of you this evening; that God has given you your partner and that

He has a plan for you both and together you will figure out..."Why us?"

God, Do It Your Way

by Katherine and James McKenna

WE CAN'T BELIEVE a year has gone by since we last attended St. Brigid's infertility Mass. Little did we know last year that we would begin a remarkable journey into re-examining our faith, and St. Gerard's words "God, do it your way," would come to have meaning.

We sat here last year, among many others, with the hopes that somehow a miracle would happen through St. Gerard's blessing. We were very wary about attending last year's Mass because, embarrassed as we are to say, we were angry at St. Gerard. Two years prior we had become pregnant and were given a St. Gerard medal to wear to protect our pregnancy. Even our parish was named St. Gerard.

We remember the joy we had when we were able to thank God for His blessing at that time. But, we miscarried on April 6th (coincidentally, St. Gerard's birthday). We were angry at St. Gerard. He was supposed to protect our pregnancy. I took the medal off and placed it in a drawer. I never wanted to wear it again. In grief, I went to our pastor for consolation. I told him of my anger. He started to tell me how fortunate I was to be in St. Gerard's parish because he could tell me about the message of St. Gerard. The message was that St. Gerard was very patient in his faith and accepted good and bad things in life as part of God's plan for him. This did not all sink in and was not what I wanted to hear. My pastor gave me his business card and wrote the words of St. Gerard on the back of it, "God, Do It Your Way" and told me to keep it in my wallet and someday I would understand. Hogwash, I thought. I want to be in control. I left feeling even more confused. I just wanted someone to tell me I would conceive and carry to term.

Our faith in God was at its lowest; our lives felt so out of control. We were not sure that we could endure. The pain of miscarrying was enough, but then to have two years go by without conceiving after the miscarriage brought us to our lowest. Our friends, Steve and Colleen, told us about last year's Mass at St. Brigid's and invited us to attend. As I had mentioned earlier, we were very wary, but somehow I drew on my faith reserve, and pulled out St. Gerard's medal again. Well, we did not become pregnant. Our friends did. How could this be happening? Does God love us? We were at the Mass, too. We were devastated.

To top everything off, the doctors felt we needed in-vitro fertilization to conceive. So, 1997 began with new hopes that in-vitro fertilization would be our miracle. We tried one fresh and one frozen cycle, both of which failed. The doctors told us we were young and we should try again, that we had a good chance. By this time we had had enough. We had reached our threshold. The words of hope from the doctors were very confusing.

It was at this point that we said, "All right God what is it that you want for us?" Do we keep trying with the doctors or do we surrender to you?" Now in a new parish, I sought consolation from my pastor. I took all our years of anger and laid it out on the table, and I quickly realized (with the guidance of my pastor) that I was tired of being angry. I wanted to be happy again. I wanted to see the joy in life, and I could not do that without God in our lives. A primary focus on becoming pregnant was taking the joy out of our lives. I quickly remembered the message from last year's infertility Mass that we should be thankful for our spouse, one of the greatest gifts from God. At that point, my husband and I let go of the anger and let God back into our lives. We grew even closer to one another, realizing that we are all we have. If a baby should come along that would be great and would certainly add to our lives. Somehow, letting go of the control and surrendering to God seemed a lot easier now. We were at peace. We decided to stop medical treatment and pursued adoption.

Well, on the anniversary of last year's Mass at St. Brigid's, my husband and I are glad to say a miracle did happen. No, we did not become pregnant—we became parents. Through the miracle of adoption, we have a one month old son, whom we named Neil Riley. Words cannot express the joy we have in our hearts for our son and most of all, for God. I feel proud to wear St. Gerard's medal, the medal of honor many mothers wear who are carrying a child. For I wear it with a different message. A message which carries a mystery that I feel fortunate enough to understand and have experienced in my life, "God, do it your way." Thank you God and St. Gerard.

Published by Resurrection Press

A Rachel Rosary *Larry Kupferman*	$3.95
Catholic Is Wonderful *Mitch Finley*	$4.95
Christian Marriage *John & Therese Boucher*	$3.95
Come, Celebrate Jesus! *Francis X. Gaeta*	$4.95
From Holy Hour to Happy Hour *Francis X. Gaeta*	$7.95
Healing through the Mass *Robert DeGrandis, SSJ*	$7.95
Healing the Wounds of Emotional Abuse *Nancy Benvenga*	$6.95
Healing Your Grief *Ruthann Williams, OP*	$7.95
Living Each Day by the Power of Faith *Barbara Ryan*	$8.95
Inwords *Mary Kraemer, OSF*	$4.50
The Healing of the Religious Life *Faricy/Blackborow*	$6.95
The Joy of Being a Catechist *Gloria Durka*	$4.50
The Joy of Being a Eucharistic Minister *Mitch Finley*	$4.95
Transformed by Love *Margaret Magdalen, CSMV*	$5.95
RVC Liturgical Series: The Liturgy of the Hours	$3.95
The Lector's Ministry	$3.95
Behold the Man *Judy Marley, SFO*	$4.50
Lights in the Darkness *Ave Clark, O.P.*	$8.95
Practicing the Prayer of Presence *van Kaam/Muto*	$7.95
5-Minute Miracles *Linda Schubert*	$3.95
Nothing but Love *Robert Lauder*	$3.95
Healthy and Holy under Stress *van Kaam/Muto*	$3.95
Season of New Beginnings *Mitch Finley*	$4.50
Season of Promises *Mitch Finley*	$4.50
Soup Pot *Ethel Pochocki*	$8.95
Stay with Us *John Mullin, SJ*	$3.95
Surprising Mary *Mitch Finley*	$7.95

For a free catalog call 1-800-892-6657